Tintern Abbey

David M. Robinson BSc, PhD, FSA

Ruins in a Wooded Valley

'After passing a miserable row of cottages, and forcing our way through a crowd of importunate beggars, we stopped to examine the rich architecture of the west front; but the door being suddenly opened, the inside perspective of the church called forth an instantaneous burst of admiration, and filled me with delight, such as I scarcely ever before experienced on a similar occasion'.

William Coxe, *An Historical Tour in Monmouthshire* (London 1801).

Tintern is among the loveliest and best-known monastic sites in the whole of the British Isles. Much of the abbey's great charm rests in its remote and striking setting, amid Wordsworth's 'steep and lofty cliffs', on the banks of his 'sylvan Wye'. Writing at the turn of the eighteenth century, William Coxe (1747–1828) was far from alone in his admiration for the celebrated ruins. The archdeacon's account of first impressions on entering the great abbey church echoes sentiments expressed time and again by his contemporary Georgian tourists. Nor was that scene greeting Coxe on his arrival by any means out of the ordinary. By the 1790s, Tintern had become a bustling tourist attraction, where — as in some latter-day eastern bazaar — beggars and would-be guides touted visitors arriving by road, or more often on boat excursions taken down the Wye from Monmouth. For several decades, the ivy-covered walls of the majestic ruins had been caught up in a widespread 'Romantic' vision of the past. Speculation concerning the history of the abbey there may have been, but this was secondary to Tintern's role as a focus of sentimental observation, an inspiration to poets, and above all a subject for artists seeking the then popular notion of the 'Picturesque'.

For the modern visitor, arriving more than two centuries after Coxe, Tintern offers scarcely a less breathtaking sight. The beggars and ivy have long disappeared, and alas boats are no longer used for excursions on the swirling brown waters of the Wye. But even so, sweeping around a road bend from Chepstow or from Monmouth, that first glimpse of the ruins seldom fails to impress. The walls and arches rising from the narrow valley floor, surrounded by a tree-covered landscape of perfectly wild natural beauty, present a scene but rarely surpassed in these islands.

Nowadays, we are perhaps rather more curious than the early tourists of the eighteenth century; we ask more questions. Principally, we will wish to know precisely when and why the abbey was built. We might also speculate upon the nature of the community which chose to settle in this comparatively remote wooded valley, and wonder about the day-to-day life within the various parts of the building. And, of course, we will ask why the abbey was abandoned and allowed to fall into ruin. These and other questions frequently asked about Tintern are addressed through the content of this guide.

A thirteenth-century manuscript illustration of a Cistercian monk, from an English chronicle that records the foundation of Cîteaux in 1098 (© The British Library Board, Cotton Nero Ms. D II, f. 108).

Opposite: 'You will find among the woods something you never found in books', wrote the Cistercian father, Bernard of Clairvaux (p. 6): Tintern Abbey seen from the Devil's Pulpit.

anit bernard chapelains de la
vierge marie descendy de la mai
son des wir de bourgongne et

Tintern and the Cistercians

Founded in 1131, Tintern Abbey was the first Cistercian monastery to be established in Wales. Just over three decades earlier, the seeds of the Cistercian adventure had been sown in a remote corner of Burgundy in eastern France. It was to prove an adventure without parallel in western Christendom, a story of rapid and extraordinary success, and one of the most remarkable phenomena in the life of the medieval Church.

To understand the monastic spirit at Tintern, we must look first at the source of fuel which inspired it. This single Welsh house was but one branch on the vast Cistercian family tree. The family traits infused every aspect of daily life at the abbey from its very foundation. The initial community of monks arrived from an influential 'mother house' located in north-central France, and Tintern was to remain a centre of monastic life and prayer for some 400 years. The Cistercians were finally forced to abandon the abbey at its suppression in 1536.

Benedict's *Rule*: A Vision of Monastic Life

Christian monasticism emerged in the deserts of Egypt and Palestine, more than 800 years before the foundation of Tintern Abbey. But in looking for the patriarch of monastic life in the West, we must turn to sixth-century Italy. Here, at the hilltop monastery of Monte Cassino south of Rome, soon after AD 535 Benedict of Nursia compiled a *Rule* setting out an orderly and practical plan for the life and organization of a monastic community. Although it was never the only model available to religious communities seeking an ideal form of communal existence, progressively the *Rule of St Benedict* gained wide currency across western Europe. Such was its prominence from the early ninth century, it could be regarded as the basis for all traditional monasticism.

In Anglo-Saxon England, from around 600 onwards, the *Rule of St Benedict* certainly played a significant part in shaping the lives of the monks, though its influence sat alongside other customs and traditions. By the ninth century, however, English monasticism was in something of a moribund state. Internal decline, coupled with catastrophic setbacks inflicted during the Viking invasions, had led to a miserable hiatus, even if the extent of this has sometimes been exaggerated. In any case, from about 940, southern Britain was to witness a remarkable monastic revolution. By the time of the Norman Conquest, there were almost forty independent and broadly wealthy 'Benedictine' religious houses concentrated in the English midlands and south.

The extent to which the traditions of monasticism in pre-Conquest Wales would be recognized alongside these English and Continental developments is debatable. Although the Welsh mother or *clas* churches were in essence 'monastic', they could certainly not be compared to the reformed Benedictine houses of pre-Conquest England. Indeed, they may have had more in common with Anglo-Saxon 'minsters'. Both were ancient institutions, where the clergy was less bound by any form of rule, and both often provided pastoral care for the surrounding population. It is notable, too, that Benedictine monasticism failed to take root in Wales until the arrival of the Normans in the late eleventh century.

Birth of the Cistercian Order

Not all monks would make saints. Almost inevitably, standards of discipline and devotion were to vary among the Benedictine abbeys of Europe. And it was a dissatisfaction with established monastic regimes that led to periodic attempts at reform. One early centre of revival was the great French

St Benedict of Nursia — the father of western monasticism. In this manuscript illumination of 1173, the saint holds a copy of his Rule, written soon after AD 535. The manuscript comes from the Cistercian abbey at Zwettl in Austria (Stiftsbibliothek Zwettl, Ms. 10, f. 46r).

Opposite: Cistercian monks arrive to colonize a new foundation, a pattern repeated across Europe through the twelfth century. This fifteenth-century 'history picture' in fact depicts St Bernard arriving at Clairvaux with his monks in 1115 (© The British Library Board, Yates Thompson Ms. 32, f. 9v).

'A place of horror and of vast solitude': the site of Robert of Molesme's Novum Monasterium, south of Dijon in Burgundy. Established in 1098, the abbey became known as Cîteaux and was the mother house of the entire Cistercian order (David Robinson).

St Stephen Harding (d. 1133), the man who gave legislative shape to the Cistercian order, in a manuscript illustration of about 1125 (Bibliothèque Municipale, Dijon, Ms. 130, f. 104).

abbey of Cluny, situated near Macon (Saône-et-Loire). Founded in 910, this was a house at first insistent upon a stricter observance of the *Rule of St Benedict.* Its rise heralded a new dawn, and it was to become the head of a vast congregation of hundreds of affiliated houses located across Europe. Yet in time critics were to round on Cluny's aristocratic brand of monasticism.

In the late eleventh and twelfth centuries, a slowly swelling tide of reform broke into open flood. Europe was to witness an unprecedented monastic renaissance, with a dramatic proliferation of new religious orders. The founding fathers of the communities born at this time were once more determined to correct abuses and to return to the simplicity of Benedict's *Rule.* Often they were inspirational dreamers, yearning for solitude, and intent upon finding a yet purer form of monastic life and observance. Many, like John of Fécamp (d. 1078), sought to dust off the beliefs of the earliest monastic fathers; theirs was a quest for the 'lovely desert … the dwelling place of lovers of God'.

It was in 1098 that one such malcontent, Abbot Robert of Molesme (d. 1110), chose to quit the prosperous Burgundian abbey he had founded just over two decades earlier, taking with him a group of some twenty-one like-minded brothers. Among their motivations and intentions, Robert and his followers were determined to seek out a physically austere location, one where they might 'live more strictly and perfectly according to the *Rule* of the most blessed Benedict'. Robert's early career as a leader of ascetics was full of restlessness, and once again he felt the need to move on. He was to lead his party of dissident

monks to a marshy and forested 'desert' south of Dijon. At a location graphically remembered by subsequent generations as 'a place of horror and of vast solitude', they set up the *Novum Monasterium* (the New Monastery). Later it took the Latin name *Cistercium,* a word derived from its marshy location. Today we know the place as Cîteaux.

Robert himself was persuaded to return to Molesme, and care of the fledgling community was left in the hands of his successor, Alberic (d. 1109). The third abbot, Stephen Harding (d. 1133), was an Englishman, widely acknowledged as the leader who gave legislative shape to the spiritual ideals of the Cîteaux experiment. To begin with, Stephen's insistence upon a course of extreme austerity pushed the poverty-stricken house to the brink of destruction. Gradually, however, the tide began to turn. With grants of land received and new recruits arriving, by 1113 Cîteaux was in a position to establish its first daughter colony, at La Ferté (Saône-et-Loire). In the longer term, too, Stephen's was the rare vision and constructive genius which provided a solid platform for the expansion and success of the emerging Cistercian order.

In the same year as the foundation of La Ferté, Cîteaux's fortunes were further transformed when the young nobleman, Bernard of Fontaines, sought admittance to the noviciate with a significant group of followers. Two years later, in 1115, the charismatic Bernard was appointed abbot of a further new daughter house at Clairvaux (Aube). From here he became the movement's arch-propagandist, taking a major role in the creation of a Cistercian identity. A persuasive and eloquent preacher, who somehow personified the monastic ideal, for more than three decades Bernard was in regular correspondence with popes, kings and bishops. Such was his universal fame and influence, by the time of his death in 1153 there were some 340 Cistercian abbeys scattered across most parts of Europe, more than 180 of which were affiliated to Clairvaux. These figures not only included brand new colonies, but also several groups of hitherto independent congregations incorporated within the Cistercian family, notably those headed by the French abbeys of Cadouin (Dordogne), Obazine (Corrèze) and Savigny (Manche).

Cistercian Ideals

After much scholarly debate, it is now widely appreciated that it would be wholly wrong to think of the creation of a fully fledged Cistercian philosophy springing from a single mind during the events of 1098. Indeed, the Cistercian constitution, and with it the movement's self-identity and its emergence as a distinct monastic *order*, was something which developed gradually over the years, partly in response to changing circumstances. Nevertheless, for William of Malmesbury, writing around 1124, the Cistercians were already 'a model for all monks', their way of life representing 'the surest road to heaven'.

Two early documents, in particular, set out the spirit of the Cistercian monastic life and its governance. Both date, in their primary form, to the abbacy of Stephen Harding. The *Exordium Parvum* was perhaps first written about 1113, and served as an authoritative account of the origins of Cîteaux for the benefit of a new generation of monks. Alongside it stands the legislative *Carta Caritatis* (Charter of Charity), a document approved and confirmed by Pope Calixtus II in 1119. This small masterpiece of prose, clarity, and good sense provided the basic machinery for maintaining a uniformity of observance at all abbeys.

Both of these sources articulate the importance of a close adherence to the *Rule of St Benedict*. As William of Malmesbury tells us, the Cistercians thought 'no jot nor tittle of it should be disregarded'. But to further underline their particular brand of monasticism, the order's founding fathers developed a series of customary observances and practices. These were formalized by the order's governing body, known as the General Chapter, in a series of statutes (or *Capitula* and *Instituta*), and so there emerged a growing body of regulations. In sum, the Cistercians came to be distinctive not just in their constitutional and legislative framework, but in almost every facet of the monastic life, including matters such as vocation and recruitment, art and architecture, and estate management.

Fundamentally, the Cistercians placed an uncompromising insistence upon poverty, rejecting all sources of luxury and wealth. To ensure the seclusion essential for true contemplation, just as at Cîteaux, abbeys were to be sited in isolation away from towns and villages, 'far from the concourse of men'. The cult of poverty and simplicity extended to their dress. Rejecting the refined black robes of the Benedictines,

St Bernard of Clairvaux (d.1153) — 'a strenuous worker at the business of God' — became the driving force behind the growth and expansion of the Cistercian order. This image of the saint is from an altarpiece of about 1290 (Museu de Mallorca).

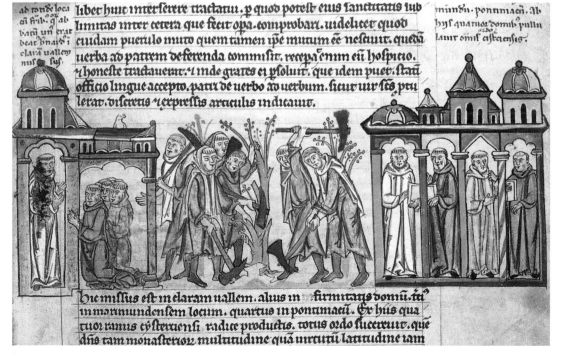

In this thirteenth-century English manuscript illustration, Stephen Harding, on the left, commissions a group of monks to found new abbeys, and to the right, the abbots of La Ferté, Clairvaux, Pontigny and Morimond are shown within their churches. The group of working monks at the centre reminds us of the importance of manual labour in the early Cistercian ideal (Cambridge University Library, Ms. Mm.5.31, f. 113r).

they chose to wear habits of coarse undyed wool, giving rise to their common identification as the 'white monks'. They rejected undershirts and breeches, followed a strict rule of silence, and at first survived on a comparatively meagre vegetarian diet.

Cistercian churches were to be plain and devoid of all ornament, their services were to be stripped of all liturgical intricacies, and even their singing was to be kept at a discreet pitch. New abbeys could only be established under carefully laid down conditions. Most were founded as colonies, or daughters, of existing houses and were to comprise at least twelve monks with an abbot. Supervision was maintained across the emerging order through a mutual system of visitation among mother and daughter houses, even if in different countries. In addition, all abbots were required to attend the annual General Chapter meeting at Cîteaux.

Choir Monks and Lay Brothers

Cistercian choir monks in a chapter meeting. The choir monks were generally educated men from noble families. This fifteenth-century manuscript illustration depicts St Bernard at Clairvaux (Musée Condé, Chantilly, Ms. 71, f. 36).

St Benedict's *Rule* had made time in the monastic day for manual work (*opus manuum*), but as the services in the older Benedictine and Cluniac houses had become richer and more complex, this aspect of daily life was progressively overlooked.

The Cistercians chose to prune back the liturgy, and to follow the offices in the basic form ordained by the saint. They restored the importance of manual work to the monastic life, which in turn was to have a profound effect on the nature of their communities.

During the formative years of the twelfth and thirteenth centuries, life within a Cistercian monastery could almost be seen as falling into two halves. Where practical, the white monks chose to avoid the customary feudal sources of revenue such as church tithes, manors, mills and rents, and therefore the intensive cultivation of agricultural land was as much an economic necessity, as it was an essential facet of the Cistercian monastic life. But it was in the further stage of providing a labour supply to undertake this work that the order proved so revolutionary.

Although the choir monks undertook some manual work, the greater part of the heavy agricultural labour was undertaken by lay brothers, or *conversi*. Other orders had turned to lay brethren in the past, but on nothing like the scale developed by the Cistercians from the mid-twelfth century. Being illiterate, and required by their specific rule book (the *Usus Conversorum*) to remain so, the *conversi* made their contribution to religion through their labour. During the twelfth century they arrived in huge armies at abbey gateways, often outnumbering the choir monks by two or three to one. Some lay brothers worked in the immediate vicinity of the abbey. Others travelled to work on outlying estates, usually within a day's journey, where lands had been acquired and organized into characteristic Cistercian farms, known as granges (p. 13).

At the abbey, the lay brothers lived as part of the full community, though they were bound by less severe rules. This division between choir monks and *conversi* had powerful influences upon the architectural arrangement of Cistercian monasteries.

The Cistercians in Britain

In all essentials, the order was well established when, in 1128, Bishop William Giffard of Winchester (1107–29) brought the first Cistercian colony to England. The site chosen was at Waverley in Surrey, with the founding monks coming from the abbey of l'Aumône (Loir-et-Cher), itself a daughter of Burgundian Cîteaux, and known as 'Petit-Cîteaux'. Although Waverley was to

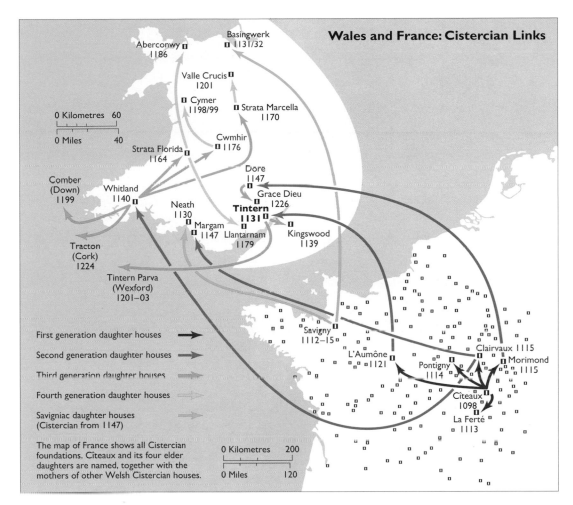

Wales and France: Cistercian Links

Aberconwy ☐ 1186
Basingwerk ☐ 1131/32
Valle Crucis ☐ 1201
☐ Cymer 1198/99
☐ Strata Marcella 1170
Cwmhir ☐ 1176
Strata Florida ☐ 1164
Dore 1147 ☐
Comber (Down) 1199
Whitland 1140 ☐
Neath 1130 ☐
Grace Dieu ☐ 1226
Tintern 1131 ☐
☐ Margam 1147 Llantarnam 1179
Kingswood 1139
Tracton (Cork) 1224
Tintern Parva (Wexford) 1201–03

0 Kilometres 60
0 Miles 40

Savigny 1112–15
L'Aumône 1121
Clairvaux 1115
Pontigny 1114
Morimond 1115
Cîteaux 1098
La Ferté 1113

First generation daughter houses →
Second generation daughter houses →
Third generation daughter houses →
Fourth generation daughter houses →
Savigniac daughter houses (Cistercian from 1147) →

The map of France shows all Cistercian foundations. Cîteaux and its four elder daughters are named, together with the mothers of other Welsh Cistercian houses.

0 Kilometres 200
0 Miles 120

Waverley Abbey: the first Cistercian colony in England, founded by Bishop William Giffard of Winchester in 1128.

Margam Abbey: founded in 1147 by the Anglo-Norman lord, Earl Robert of Gloucester (d. 1147).

Valle Crucis Abbey: founded in 1201 by the Welsh prince, Madog ap Gruffudd Maelor (d. 1236).

become the mother of an important group of houses in southern England, it was Yorkshire which proved the true cradle-land of Cistercian success in Britain. The systematic colonization of northern England and Scotland was initiated by St Bernard himself, and began with the foundation of Rievaulx Abbey in 1132. By the end of the reign of King Stephen (1154) there were almost fifty new foundations, including thirteen houses incorporated from the congregation of Savigny in 1147.

Wales, too, like the north of England, was to prove particularly attractive to the white monks. Apart from Tintern, and the two Welsh Savigniac houses (Neath and Basingwerk), ten more abbeys were eventually established. The course of their foundation and history can virtually be seen in two distinct streams. On the one hand, those of the south and east (including Tintern, Margam, and Neath) were founded by the Anglo-Norman conquerors, and

their subsequent fortunes were largely dependent upon later Marcher lords. In contrast, the other stream flowed through the heartland of Wales. And here it was St Bernard's Clairvaux which was destined to be the fount of the Welsh Cistercian triumph. It began with the foundation of Whitland in 1140, and included the houses at Strata Florida, Aberconwy, and Valle Crucis. White monk monasticism was at home in the terrain of north and west Wales; its prosperity was assured by its appeal to the native princes of these regions.

'The story spread everywhere', a thirteenth-century chronicler was moved to record, 'that men of outstanding holiness and perfect religion had come from a far land'. 'Thus very soon', he tells us, 'they grew into a great company'. In all, there were eventually some eighty-six Cistercian monasteries located across the length and breadth of Britain.

A History of the Abbey

Foundation

Tintern Abbey was founded by Walter fitz Richard of Clare (d. 1137/38), the Anglo-Norman lord of Chepstow, on 9 May 1131. It was only the second white monk colony to be established anywhere in the British Isles, and was the very first in Wales. However, it was not the earliest Norman monastery on this part of the Welsh border. Over the previous half century and more, the conquerors had chosen to back a cause with which they were familiar. They had introduced a whole clutch of Benedictine priories, which had nearly always been founded as dependencies of large abbeys in England or in France. 'Black monk' houses nestled in the shadow of Norman strongholds, on the fringes of the embryonic boroughs at Chepstow, at Monmouth, at Abergavenny, and elsewhere.

But Walter of Clare was of a new generation. He was also related by marriage to Bishop William of Winchester, who had given the white monks their earliest British foothold, at Waverley in Surrey in 1128. Having resolved to bring the Cistercians to his lordship of Chepstow, Walter followed the path taken by his kinsman. He looked to the abbey of l'Aumône, in the diocese of Chartres, to provide the founding colony of monks (p. 8).

Given that l'Aumône was in turn a daughter of Cîteaux, Tintern was linked as a granddaughter to the Burgundian mother house. The abbot of l'Aumône would have been entitled to make an annual visit to his daughter, and there are documented contacts (if infrequent) through to 1330. Each year, as instructed through the *Carta Caritatis*, the abbot of Tintern would have been required to attend the General Chapter at Cîteaux.

Twelfth-Century Growth

The heavily wooded slopes bordering the river Wye would certainly have met the criteria for the foundation of a Cistercian abbey. Give them 'a wilderness or forest', wrote Gerald of Wales (d. 1223) in the 1180s, 'and in a few years you will find a dignified abbey in the midst of smiling plenty'. Not that the lower Wye Valley was totally without a native population in the early twelfth century. Part of Walter of Clare's initial endowment included important property at Porthcasseg, just south of the abbey site. Lands here had earlier belonged to the church of Llandaff, and they had probably been worked long before the foundation.

Landed possessions were the very lifeblood of the new community (p. 13). Apart from Porthcasseg, Walter's grants included property at Modesgate, Penterry, and Wilcrick. Another early acquisition was at Merthyrgeryn on the Caldicot Level, and the arable grange of Trelleck was confirmed to the monks by Richard of Clare (d. 1176). In all, we must imagine the first generation of Tintern's lay brothers vigorously preparing areas for cultivation, putting up grange buildings, and felling woods to extend the available plough land. The pattern set in the first decades was to continue for several centuries. Apart from major gifts, the land-hungry monks also sought to extend and improve their estates. Smaller benefactions, exchanges, and occasional purchases all formed part of the process.

During these formative years, the brothers were led by at least one man with considerable strength of character. Abbot Henry (about 1148–57) had spent his youth as a robber, making a 'lucrative profession of brigandage'. Moved to repentance, he took the Cistercian habit and appears to have developed an intense spirituality, 'conspicuous at the altar for the abundance of his tears'. Henry is known to have visited both the pope and St Bernard.

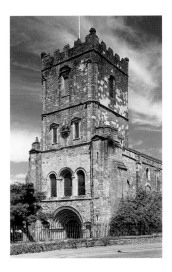

The Benedictine priory church at Chepstow. It was founded about 1070, in the first wave of the Norman conquest of south-east Wales.

Opposite: The Cistercian fathers encouraged the location of abbeys 'far from the concourse of men'. For the community at Tintern, the remote location of the house in the steep-sided valley of the Wye would have provided 'a kind of second paradise of wooded delight'. A view of the abbey church from the north-east.

*William Marshal the younger,
second earl of Pembroke
(d. 1231), was one of Tintern's
most liberal benefactors. His gifts
may have allowed for extensive
building works at the abbey in
the first half of the thirteenth
century. William was buried in
the Temple Church in London,
where this effigy is generally
attributed to him.*

*Right: Tintern's first daughter
house was founded at Kingswood
in Gloucestershire in 1139.
All that remains is this mid-
fifteenth-century gatehouse
(English Heritage).*

*Far right: Tintern's second
daughter house was founded
by William Marshal (d. 1219)
in 1201–03, at Tintern Parva in
Co. Wexford, Ireland (George
Munday/Design Pics/Getty Images).*

Abbot William's time at Tintern (about 1169–88) was less happy. The house was in dispute with its sister at Waverley, and William's career ended abruptly in 1188 when he resigned after meeting visitors sent by the General Chapter of the order. About this same time, Tintern first departed from the ideals of the General Chapter statutes in receiving a grant of ecclesiastical tithes from the church of Woolaston and the chapel of Alvington in Gloucestershire.

Daughter Houses

A clear sign of Tintern's early success was its ability to attract local recruits to the noviciate. Within eight years of its own foundation, the abbey was in a position to colonize a daughter house. In 1139, Kingswood in Gloucestershire was founded by William of Berkeley, with Prior Thomas of Tintern chosen to become the first abbot of the new house.

In 1189, the illustrious William Marshal (d. 1219) became lord of Chepstow and patron of Tintern; by 1199 he was earl of Pembroke. In addition to his extensive estates in south Wales, Earl William was also lord of Leinster in south-east Ireland. Caught in a storm on the Irish Sea in 1201, the earl struck a bargain with God: he vowed to establish a new abbey if saved from shipwreck. So it was that a second colony of monks was drawn from Tintern, journeying to Ireland, and settling at Tintern Parva (Little Tintern) by 1203. The Marshal's Irish Tintern, west of Wexford, was also known as *de Voto*, the abbey of the vow.

The Thirteenth Century

As earls of Pembroke, William Marshal's heirs continued to support the Welsh house. William the younger (d. 1231) was particularly generous in the fullness of his confirmation of all earlier gifts. In 1223–24, he added lands north-west of Usk which were to form the basis of the grange at Estavarney, or Monkswood. William also granted Tintern its important arable property at Rogerstone. In return, the monks were to maintain a lamp burning at the tomb of his mother, Isabel, countess of Pembroke.

Although the Cistercian statutes set out clear restrictions on the burial of lay persons within Cistercian abbeys, founders and their successors generally expected to be honourably interred within monasteries of their patronage. For the monks, lamps or a regular Mass for the soul of the patron meant additional lands or income. At Tintern, the burial of Isabel Marshal in 1220 was unlikely to have been the first such arrangement. Later, two of her sons, Walter and Anselm were laid to rest at the abbey in 1245, and her daughter Maud was buried there in 1248.

An extensive rebuilding programme in the first half of the thirteenth century (pp. 29–31) would have meant keeping a close eye on estate profits. Indeed, the gifts from William Marshal the younger were perhaps earmarked to support the work. As things were progressing, Tintern was blessed with another leader of note. Abbot Ralph (about 1232–45), we are told, was 'a man gifted in no small way with sobriety of habits, and splendour of wisdom'.

The Abbey's Estates

Land was by far the most important economic resource for twelfth-century monasteries. For the Cistercians, forbidden many of the sources of revenue available to black monk abbeys, there was little choice: 'plough or perish, dig or die'. In this respect, Tintern was placed on a reasonably sound economic footing by its founder, with property granted on both sides of the Wye. Additional lands were granted by later benefactors.

Wherever possible, these landed estates were early organized into compact farms known as granges. The grange was, in fact, the key to successful Cistercian land management. Tintern held at least twelve such properties, of which Estavarney (Monkswood), Merthyrgeryn, Moor, Rogerstone, Ruding, Secular Firmary and Trelleck lay in today's Monmouthshire, with Aluredeston (Alvington), Ashwell, Brockweir, Modesgate and Woolaston across the Wye in Gloucestershire.

The founding fathers of the Cistercian order had chosen to starve, rather than to accept gifts of manorialized or inhabited land. But such unencumbered holdings were hard to find on the twelfth-century Welsh border, even in the comparative remoteness of the Wye Valley. Walter of Clare was probably anxious to offload church property earlier grabbed by conquest, and included the manor of Porthcasseg with his original endowment to the Tintern monks. The community had little choice but to accept, as was true of his gift of Woolaston manor. They made efforts to carve consolidated granges within the bounds of each, but they were never entirely free of responsibility for serfs and tenants. The abbey was to hold a central court for all its tenants west of the Wye at Porthcasseg. Fines were levied, and manorial justice dispensed.

Much of Tintern's land was probably considered marginal in the twelfth and early thirteenth centuries. This was the way the Cistercians would have wanted it. From a very early date Tintern was busy extending and improving its agricultural holdings, cutting down woodland, and draining marsh on the Monmouthshire Levels. The monks also exchanged quite sizeable chunks of property in order to bring their estates closer together for more efficient management. The brothers also had a discerning eye for a balanced agricultural economy. Trelleck and Rogerstone were important arable granges, whereas at Moor there may have been a greater emphasis on pastoralism.

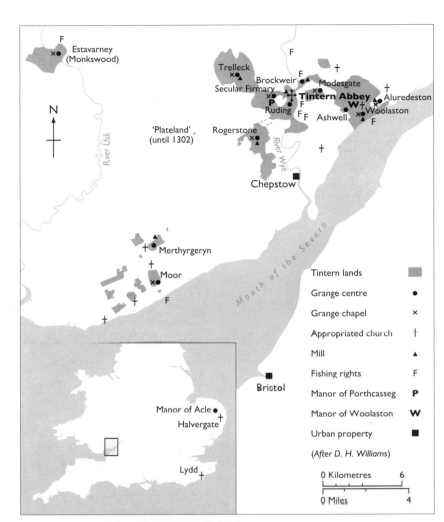

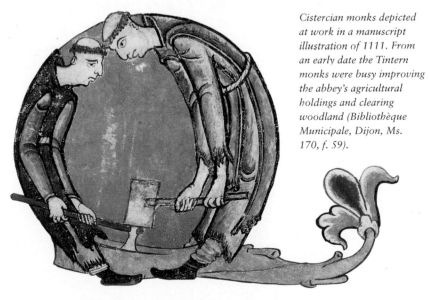

Cistercian monks depicted at work in a manuscript illustration of 1111. From an early date the Tintern monks were busy improving the abbey's agricultural holdings and clearing woodland (Bibliothèque Municipale, Dijon, Ms. 170, f. 59).

Roger Bigod, fifth earl of Norfolk (d. 1306), was eventually to prove a munificent benefactor to the Tintern monks, and was remembered by later generations as the 'Founder'. This is an impression of the earl's seal (The National Archives: PRO, E 26/1 seal 78).

Pressure to improve and extend the abbey's arable estate continued through the century. About 1245, the monks were granted permission to drain and ditch 'their grange in the moor of Magor' and to do with it 'as they see fit'. Woodland clearance, or assarting, was also continuing. Small parcels of wood were being cleared in the manor of Porthcasseg, and in 1282 the abbey was fined the very heavy sum of £112 for felling 200 acres (81ha) of royal forest at Woolaston without licence.

Some idea of the relative wealth Tintern had achieved by the close of the century comes from a papal taxation document of 1291, known as the *Taxatio Ecclesiastica*. At the time, the monks were farming well over 3,000 acres (1,214ha) of arable land on the Welsh side of the Wye. On their pastures there were some 3,264 sheep, and from another source we know the wool was of the finest quality. As a whole, the abbey's possessions were assessed at just over £145, by no means vast when compared to many English monasteries, but sufficient to make Tintern the fifth wealthiest religious house in Wales.

A Second Founder: Roger Bigod, Earl of Norfolk

In 1245–46, through the Marshal heiress Maud (d. 1248), the lordship of Chepstow had passed to the Bigod family, earls of Norfolk. Maud's grandson, Roger Bigod, fifth earl of Norfolk (1270–1306), inherited the office of marshal of England. He was, until his fall from grace in 1297, one of the most powerful figures at the court of King Edward I (1272–1307).

Apart from his extensive rebuilding at Chepstow Castle, Bigod was eventually to take a keen interest in the patronage of Tintern. Later generations of monks were to remember him in particular as the builder of their abbey church, though he is most unlikely to have been involved in the very earliest stages of the programme, initiated in 1269 (p. 32). The first signs of his effective support are perhaps represented by the grant of the church at Halvergate in Norfolk, possibly before 1279. But for the hard evidence of the earl's

The Monks at Tintern

A grave slab of one of Tintern's abbots, drawn about 1820 by David ap Thomas Powell. When first discovered, in 1756, there were extensive traces of gilding around the abbot's head. The slab fragment still survives, and perhaps dates from about 1300. It is tempting to think that it represents Abbot Ralph (about 1294–1305), who oversaw completion of Tintern's great Gothic church around the beginning of the fourteenth century (Cardiff Central Library).

An abbot accompanied by at least twelve choir monks would have been sent out from l'Aumône in 1131 to colonize the new abbey at Tintern. The founding community would also have included a party of lay brothers (*conversi*). Despite the French origins of the community, novices were soon recruited locally. Indeed, Tintern may have had up to sixty monks by the time the first daughter house was established at Kingswood in 1139.

The earliest documented record for the number of brothers dates from 1395. In that year, fourteen monks and their abbot witnessed a charter. In 1536, at the time of the suppression, the community was still thirteen strong.

The names of some 100 monks are known from the four centuries of monastic life. Twenty-three of these became abbots of Tintern. The vast majority of the abbey's monks were of Anglo-Norman or English origin. The most common names were Thomas and William, followed by Walter and Nicholas. Tintern also had the only two Cistercian Edwards known from Wales.

The valuable tithes from the church at Lydd in Kent were first acquired by Tintern from the Italian abbey of Santa Maria de Gloria — of the order of Flora, in the diocese of Anagni — in 1326–27. The church, seen here from the south, was largely built in the thirteenth century. The tower was added in 1442–46 designed by Thomas Stanley (d. 1462), a senior mason at Canterbury Cathedral (akg-images/A. F. Kersting).

munificence, we must wait until the turn of the century. Elderly and still childless, and forced to barter with the king over the future of his estates, Bigod set aside certain insurances for the afterlife. It was in 1302 that he granted Tintern 'all his manor of Acle', situated more than 200 miles (320km) away in Norfolk. It was a particularly generous gift, amounting to the abbey's single most profitable asset, and accounting for up to one quarter of its annual income by the sixteenth century. In addition, the earl granted the monks the manor of Aluredeston (Alvington), Gloucestershire, in exchange for their property at 'Plateland' in Monmouthshire. And, for a fee, he gave them additional lands at Modesgate.

So great was Roger Bigod's munificence that later observers — notably the traveller-antiquary William Worcestre (writing in the 1470s) — considered him the abbey's founder. In 1535, a year before Tintern's suppression, the monks were still distributing alms to the poor five times a year for the repose of his soul.

Bigod had probably been on good terms with Abbot Ralph (about 1294–1305). Ralph was certainly a man in royal favour, and it is a measure of his character that he received no fewer than five summonses to Parliament between 1295 and 1305.

He was succeeded by the businesslike Hugh of Wyke (1305–20). In 1307, it was Abbot Hugh who had the foresight to dispatch Brother Edward on the long journey to Carlisle to secure royal approval of the abbey's lands and charters. Twenty-two grants were confirmed by the dying Edward I.

The opening of the fourteenth century saw the abbey reach a zenith in its fortunes. Apart from the very valuable tithes from the church of Lydd in Kent, first acquired in 1326–27, Tintern made very few significant additions to its property after this time.

The Later Middle Ages

Abbot Walter of Hereford (about 1321–27) was to receive the only known royal visitor to Tintern, Edward II (1307–27). The hapless king spent two nights as the abbot's guest in 1326. They may have talked of John de Ispannia, a one-time royal servant who had been placed in the monks' charge in 1314. The king's father, Edward I, had also sent one of his retired servants to Tintern in 1304. Both these men had been granted 'corrodies', spending their old age as monastic inmates. Indeed, the presence of

King Edward II, who stayed at Tintern in 1326, is the only known royal visitor to the abbey. The king's tomb effigy rests in Gloucester Cathedral, a Benedictine abbey church (Angelo Hornak Photograph Library).

Right: A folio from an edition of the English chronicle, the Flores Historiarum, *which records events anchored to Tintern over the years 1305 to 1323. If not a Tintern book, then these sections were certainly derived from the abbey's scriptorium (© The British Library Board, Royal Ms. 14 C. VI, f. 254).*

Below: The 1387–88 bailiff's accounts for the abbey's grange at Merthyrgeryn show that almost the entire property had been leased out to tenants (National Library of Wales, Badminton Ms. 1571).

Lucca. Building works still underway at the monastery (pp. 35–37) might have been one of the reasons for mortgaging property, or even the future wool clip, in a bid to raise hard cash.

Of greater significance was the current of widespread economic change creeping into the agricultural affairs of the abbey at this time. Tintern was by no means exceptional. Cistercian houses everywhere were being forced to abandon the ideals of grange farming, moving ever closer to a manorial system. More and more monastic land was leased out in return for regular fixed cash rents. Falling numbers of lay brothers and rises in wage prices for hired labour accelerated the process. Then, in the spring of 1349, the Black Death struck Wales.

Although we lack direct evidence, the pestilence must surely have compounded the difficulties Tintern was experiencing with labour shortages. The general trend across the abbey's estates is perhaps best summed up by the circumstances on its Merthyrgeryn holding. In 1291, this property on the edge of the coastal levels still seems to have been managed by lay brothers. By 1387–88, however, a detailed bailiff's account reveals that almost the entire grange had been leased out to tenants.

Despite the impact of the Black Death, which is known to have had serious consequences on the number of choir monks at many abbeys, Tintern maintained a sizeable community through to the end of the fourteenth century. Firm evidence comes from a document of 1395 which was witnessed by the abbot, John Wysbech (1387–1407), together with fourteen monks of his house.

Meanwhile, the trend towards an increasing secularization of the monastery's economic affairs continued. In this process, the power of the abbey cellarer was to decline markedly. In the twelfth and thirteenth centuries, he had exercised direct control over the abbey estates. His wide experience often marked him out as the obvious choice for promotion to abbot. By the fifteenth century, although the cellarer was still involved with estate matters, the reins of effective control had passed to the steward, a lay official of ever increasing importance in the abbey's affairs. In 1402, Tintern's steward was John ap Wilcock, a local landowner of no great rank. Just over a half century later the post was held by a peer of the realm.

Tintern was clearly experiencing certain financial difficulties in the early 1400s. In part, this was due

corrodians was to become a new aspect of life within the abbey during the later Middle Ages. It was not an obligation which could be taken lightly, with suitable accommodation just one consideration.

As the century progressed, several episodes hint at weaknesses in management and monastic discipline. In 1330–34, for example, there was a dispute concerning the abbey's fisheries on the Wye. Weirs had been raised to such an extent that they were restricting the passage of river traffic. Henry of Lancaster (d. 1345) complained to the king that supplies were not reaching his town and castle at Monmouth. But the monks refused to cooperate and even assaulted officials sent to lower the weirs.

A few years later, in 1340, the abbot acknowledged a debt of some £174 owed to an Italian merchant of to the damaging effects of the Welsh uprising under Owain Glyndŵr. In 1406, writing to the bishop of Hereford, the king noted that much of the abbey's property 'had been destroyed and consumed by the Welsh rebels'.

Pilgrim offerings were one source of cash relief. The monks claimed to possess a miraculous image of the Virgin which, despite attempts, could not be removed from a chapel outside the west door of the abbey church (p. 40). In 1414, it was said 'a very great multitude [already] resort to the chapel', but now Pope John XXII was to grant an indulgence to all those who were to visit on certain feast days, 'and give alms'.

In the 1450s it was Sir William Herbert of Raglan who was serving as the abbey's steward. In 1468 he became earl of Pembroke, and a year later was buried at Tintern following his execution after the battle of Edgecote. In his will, the earl made provision for the building of his tomb, and offered any surplus in the endowment 'to build new cloisters' (pp. 36–37).

In the late fifteenth century, this part of the Wye Valley would have presented a very different scene from that encountered by the earliest Cistercian brothers in the 1130s. The appearance of Chapel Hill and the adjacent Angidy Valley had changed quite dramatically. A settled community had long since emerged. Cottages were built up to the very shadow of the precinct wall, and there are clear indications of bustling commercial activity. Licences were granted to tenant shopkeepers who wished to set up stalls and taverns to sell their bread, beer, meat and other merchandise. The rights were guarded, and fines were levied on those who tried peddling their wares without the abbot's permission.

In the last half century of monastic life, injunctions arising from the abbey's court at Porthcasseg further testify to the expanding local population. In 1528, for example, it was necessary to pass a regulation preventing the playing of dice and cards throughout the lordship. Another prohibited the playing of handball within the gate of the monastery.

The monks continued to play host to corrodians or pensioners who had purchased the right to spend their old age as inmates. John Owain and his wife were there from 1521, occupying a chamber 'called "the candlehouse" above the great door next to the church'. They received a gallon of better beer a day, together with a portion of meat or fish equivalent to

that eaten by one of the brothers. Servants, too, were commonplace in and about the monastic precinct. There was a porter, a launderer, a keeper of the ferry, and even a gaoler, each one probably wearing a tunic of the abbot's livery.

Suppression: The End of Monastic Life

Tintern's last abbot, Richard Wyche, took up his office in 1521. The signs of impending disaster were already close at hand. Locally, the abbey's domineering steward, Charles Somerset, earl of Worcester (d. 1526), was taking more than just a watchful interest in estate matters. Wyche sought to curb the earl's ambitions, eventually bringing a list of grievances before the influential court of Star Chamber. At much the same time, a harsher wind of change was gathering pace in the land. Archbishop Thomas Wolsey (d. 1530) was busy picking off almost thirty smaller monasteries, where it was claimed 'neither God was served nor religion kept'.

Even before the reign of King Henry VIII (1509–47), much of the spiritual drive which had stoked the fires of the monastic revival some 400 years before had been exhausted. Wolsey's suppressions in the 1520s caused no public outcry, and little

From the 1450s, the great Sir William Herbert of Raglan served as the abbey's steward. He was buried at Tintern in 1469. In his will he provided an endowment 'to build new cloisters'. This manuscript illustration of Herbert dates to about 1461–62 (© The British Library Board, Royal Ms. 18 D. II, f. 6).

King Henry VIII was at once both supreme head of the Church in his realm and a suppressor of monasteries. Henry is seen here in an illuminated initial at the opening of the Valor Ecclesiasticus, *the great survey of monastic property, 1535 (The National Archives: PRO, E 344/22).*

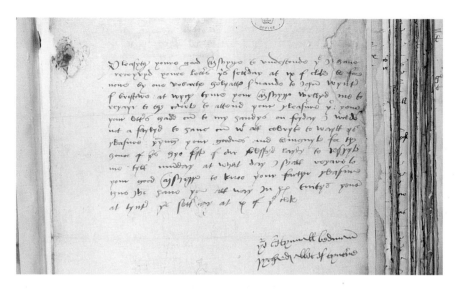

Abbot Richard Wyche's letter to Cromwell, 1534: 'begging you to respite me till Monday for honour of this high feast of our Blessed Lady' (The National Archives: PRO, SP 1/85/1133).

by way of outspoken protest from churchmen. Seen for what they were, however, his actions were to give ideas to other would-be plunderers of monastic property.

At the beginning of the 1530s, the abbeys of Wales had little capacity to withstand the force of change. Moreover, there were few people who would be prepared to resist on their behalf. Indeed, members of the gentry who stood to benefit from any disposal of monastic property were soon queuing up to ingratiate themselves with Thomas Cromwell (d. 1540), architect of the suppression of the monasteries.

The Act of Supremacy (1534) placed the king, below God, as supreme head of the Church throughout his realm. For monastic inmates, it was certainly not a time to incur royal displeasure. Thus, when in September 1534 Abbot Richard received a letter requesting him to visit Secretary Cromwell at court, he could not afford to take the proposed meeting lightly. Wyche's reply, begging to be excused for several days in order that he could keep the feast of the Nativity of the Virgin at Tintern, perhaps shows the continued strength of Cistercian spirituality.

Meanwhile, Cromwell had begun to see the financial benefits of even a partial closure of the 800 or so religious houses situated throughout England and Wales. Before any definite move, he knew the king would require a comprehensive report and valuation of their property. In January 1535, he appointed commissioners to conduct a thorough inquiry within the dioceses of England and Wales.

Henry Somerset, earl of Worcester (d. 1549), who was granted the bulk of Tintern's south Wales estates by Henry VIII. The earl's wooden tomb effigy rests in the priory church at Chepstow.

In the results of the great survey, known as the *Valor Ecclesiasticus*, the net annual income of Tintern was assessed at some £192, still small by the standards of many English houses, but sufficient to rank it as the wealthiest abbey in Wales.

A second set of commissioners was soon looking into the spiritual affairs of the monasteries. In March 1536 one of Cromwell's visitors in Wales, Dr John Vaughan, wrote to his master with hearsay evidence that Tintern was one of several houses said to be 'greatly abused'.

A few weeks later an Act was passed whereby those monasteries with fewer than twelve monks, and whose possessions could not yield a benchmark valuation in excess of £200, were to be suppressed. Around 200 houses were to disappear in 1536–37, representing the first stage in the total suppression of the monasteries, a drawn-out process which continued through to 1540.

Tintern not only had the required twelve conventual monks in 1536, but a further survey of its property yielded the higher valuation of £238. There is even a suggestion that the *Valor* figure of the previous year was deliberately falsified to bring the abbey below the threshold required for suppression. In the event, Tintern was surrendered to the king's visitors on 3 September 1536. Abbot Richard Wyche was given a pension of £23, and the twelve remaining choir monks received £8 8s. 0d. Thirty-five monastic servants were granted £16 5s. 1d.

All articles of value from the abbey were catalogued, weighed, and sent to the king's treasury. The silver and gilt plate, for example, totalled some 469 ounces (13.3kg). Other disposables such as glass, timber and less precious items were probably auctioned on the spot. Within months, the abbey buildings, along with its border possessions, were granted to Henry Somerset, earl of Worcester (d. 1549). With important castles at Chepstow and Raglan, the earl had no desire to live at Tintern, though several letters he sent to Cromwell in the second half of 1537 were dated at the site.

The destruction of the monastic buildings does not seem to have been an immediate priority. Although the lead on the roofs had been valued at £124 in 1536, some of it — at least — was being melted down by the king's plumbers as late as 1541. And later still, in 1545–46, Earl Henry was being charged £217 for lead and bells from Tintern.

The Abbey Precinct

The overall planning of Cistercian monasteries was designed to ensure the necessary seclusion and tranquillity. At Tintern, the abbey precinct comprised a series of walled enclosures and courts, with controlled entry to the various parts.

The monastery complex covered up to 27 acres (11ha), with much of it enclosed by an outer precinct wall. The wall stood up to 10 feet (3m) high: sections of it survive within garden walls on the hillside above the principal abbey buildings. We cannot be certain of its course in all areas, nor can we be sure that the wall formed a complete circuit. The alignment on the eastern side, for example, takes in a very steep slope down towards the hay meadows on the banks of the Wye.

The precinct wall was broken by at least two outer gateways. One of these stood on the south-west side, close to the point where several medieval land routes converged at the abbey. The second was situated along the river frontage. Here, the outer arch of the watergate can still be seen alongside the Anchor Hotel. The watergate led to a river slipway, with a ferry crossing giving access to the abbey's Gloucestershire holdings.

There is a record of the abbey's 'Great Gate' from 1536: the monks referred to their 'porter and keeper of our gaol'. The Great Gate may survive in part at St Anne's, a private house just inside the line of the precinct wall. On the north side of the house, there are traces of a thirteenth-century vaulted gate hall. St Anne's incorporates the remains of the gatehouse chapel.

From the gatehouses, routes led to the outer and inner courts. The outer court probably lay to the west and on the hillside to the south. It was here that the abbey's workaday buildings would have been located: barns, stables, granaries, houses for oxen and cattle, and so on. A mill was probably located on the Angidy brook, outside the precinct wall.

Access to the inner court was more restricted. This lay immediately west of the abbey church, where various ruins still survive. The substantial structure with a vaulted undercroft may have served as a high-status guest house. To the east, excavations have revealed a thirteenth-century aisled building

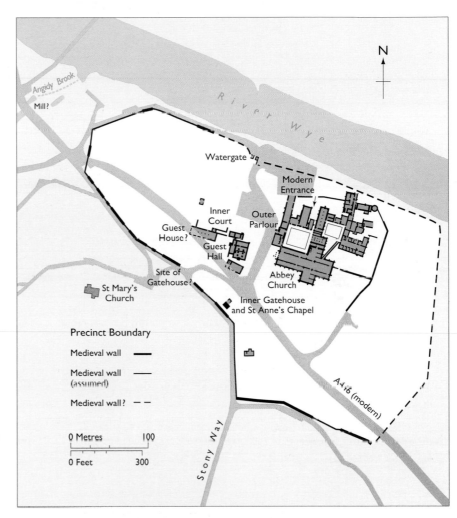

with a central open hearth. It was probably a communal guest hall. South of this, the gable end of a late medieval block stands as the most prominent surviving feature. In the later Middle Ages, parts of this inner court area were given over to metalliferous industrial activity.

At the heart of the monastery lay the abbey church and cloister buildings. Entry was gained via the porch and outer parlour (pp. 59–60). The Cistercian plan for these central buildings was remarkably uniform. It followed the customary medieval monastic outline, which was practical and made the best possible use of natural light.

Industrial Interlude

In the centuries which separate the end of monastic life at Tintern from the present day, we should remember there have been several more distinct phases in the long history of the site.

The earl of Worcester and his successors soon chose to lease out tenements and parcels of land in and around the former monastic buildings. For the poorer tenants, makeshift homes raised amid the more adaptable cloister chambers had to suffice. Any suitable structure across the precinct area (p. 19) as a whole was probably seen as ripe for conversion to a cottage. From the 1560s, new industrial opportunities at Tintern were to encourage yet further tenant occupation.

We know from archaeological excavations west of the abbey church that non-ferrous metalworking began through Cistercian enterprise in the later Middle Ages. But from 1566, a thriving industrial complex began to emerge, based on new raw materials. The production of iron wire was attracted to the site by the potential for water power from the adjacent Angidy brook, and by plentiful supplies of timber to provide furnace charcoal. The earliest furnace was known as the Laytons, and its associated forge — perhaps on the site of the abbey's home farm mill — was situated just outside the former monastic precinct, where the Angidy feeds into the Wye. By the end of the seventeenth century another furnace had come into blast, and a new forge was in production higher up the Angidy Valley. In all, furnaces, forges, mill leats and ponds, and all the associated industrial processes had transformed the abbey environs.

For the most part, with roofs gone, and windows smashed, the monastic buildings themselves had fallen into chronic decay. The ruinous structures and collapsed debris were overgrown with brambles and ivy. The abbey church, however, continued to stand virtually complete, even if it was to be put to less dignified uses. Eighteenth-century villagers were at one time using the abbey as a fives court, and the church was a place to play quoits.

In the two centuries since the departure of the Cistercians, very little interest had been shown in the monastic history of the site. The wild scenery of the Wye Valley would certainly not have appealed

to the 'Augustan' tastes of early Georgian England. Moreover the Gothic architecture of the ruins would have appeared crude alongside the classical ideals of the time. Few people would have bothered to travel specifically to view the remains of the medieval abbey.

Resurrection: The Romantics Discover Tintern

In this respect, the Buck brothers were exceptional. Their engraving of Tintern, published in 1732, is one of the earliest known depictions of the site. Although a somewhat stylistic record, it reveals the abbey church much as we see it today. In subsequent years, fashions and tastes were to change. Within decades, the wooded slopes of the Wye were to become a magnet for droves of 'Romantic' tourists, with Tintern acknowledged as a jewel and highlight of the tour.

From accounts recorded later in the century, it seems that Charles Somerset (1709–56), fourth duke of Beaufort, took a new pride in the ruins. Sometime before his death, the duke appears to have initiated steps to curb the neglect at Tintern. Up to a hundred workmen were engaged by the estate steward to clear the interior of the abbey church, then 'choked up with rubbish'. Some of the 'rubbish' was, alas, thrown into the river. The ground was levelled and turfed, and fragments of fallen masonry were heaped in ornamental piles around the piers of the nave and presbytery. An attempt was made to protect the good works from vandalism, with locking doors hung at the west front and iron gates used to close off the other principal entry points.

The Beaufort family's concern for the care of Tintern at this time cannot be explained in terms of

This engraving of Tintern, one of the earliest known depictions of the site, was published by the brothers Samuel and Nathaniel Buck in 1732 (National Library of Wales, PB 1385).

Charles Somerset (1709–56), fourth duke of Beaufort, who appears to have taken steps to protect Tintern in the 1750s (His grace the duke of Beaufort).

Opposite: This 1794 watercolour of the monk's choir and presbytery at Tintern by J. M. W. Turner (1775–1851) is one of several dramatic studies he completed of the site (Turner Bequest, Tate Gallery, London D00374).

This 1794 watercolour of Tintern Abbey by Edward Dayes (1763–1804) is one of many 'Picturesque' studies of the site (Whitworth Art Gallery, The University of Manchester).

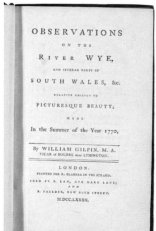

William Gilpin's influential guidebook, Observations on the River Wye, *was published in 1782 and proved an immediate 'best-seller' (National Library of Wales).*

a modern concept of conservation. The thick screen of ivy which covered most of the walls, for example, was to remain part of the attraction of the site. Nor can it be said that the clearance work was motivated by a search for antiquarian knowledge, though 'expectations were formed of finding some valuable relics'. Such growing pride in the Gothic ruins was, nevertheless, to anticipate the abbey's appeal to an ever increasing body of visitors arriving in the Wye Valley in the later eighteenth century.

Perhaps the most influential of these early tourists was the Reverend William Gilpin (1724–1804), who made his Wye river voyage in 1770. Soon after his return, Gilpin wrote to a friend enthusing that if 'you have never navigated the Wye, you have seen nothing'. The vicar's modesty meant it was to be twelve years before he published his guidebook, *Observations on the River Wye* (London 1782), though when it appeared it was to become an

immediate best-seller. Travellers began flocking to the area, with Ross as the popular town to begin their journey downriver.

The tourists paid their fare and boarded small boats laden with picnic hampers, and equipped with coverings against sun and rain. Reading their copy of Gilpin, at tables provided for drawing and writing, they were offered the principles by which they might judge the 'Picturesque' qualities of a view. They looked forward to Tintern, said by Gilpin to be 'the most beautiful' scene of all, even if he felt there was room to improve the picture-like features of the abbey church:

'Though the parts are beautiful, the whole is ill-shaped ... a number of gable-ends hurt the eye with their regularity; and disgust it by the vulgarity of their shape. A mallet judiciously used (but who durst use it?) might be of service in fracturing some of them ...'.

Such considerations did little to deter the 'Romantics' of the late Georgian era. For them, the 'Sublime' impact of the surrounding rugged terrain was just as important, stirring as it could profound feelings of astonishment and awe in heart and mind. Indeed, the Wye Valley was to become one of the most popular regions in a broad movement which led to the rediscovery of the beauty in wild landscape across Great Britain as a whole. From 1793, war with France prevented 'Romantic' travellers touring further afield to Switzerland or to the Rhine. Instead, as the Monmouth guidebook writer Charles Heath observed, the Wye was 'honoured with a very large share of Public Notice'.

One of those boarding the ferry at Bristol to begin a Wye tour in the early summer of 1792 was J. M. W. Turner (1775–1851). Barely seventeen years of age, and full of expectation, the artist was on his first true visit to Wales. The pencil sketches he made at Tintern were to provide the raw material for a magnificent selection of watercolours subsequently worked up and exhibited at the Royal Academy in 1794–95. Turner returned to the Wye Valley on several of his Welsh tours, and passed by the abbey once again in 1798.

Possibly the best-known of the late eighteenth-century 'Romantic' visitors to Tintern, however, was the poet William Wordsworth (1770–1850). In 1793 he came alone, a troubled young man of twenty-three. Five years later, in July 1798, he was to come back in happier times with his sister Dorothy. After several days touring on foot and by boat, they boarded a return ferry to Bristol. It was on the homeward journey that Wordsworth committed to memory the finishing touches for his *Lines Composed a Few Miles Above Tintern Abbey*. 'No poem of mine', he was to say afterwards, 'was composed under circumstances more pleasant for me to remember than this'.

As the new century dawned, the abbey was that bustling attraction seen by Archdeacon William Coxe (p. 3). Contemporary tourists were even choosing to enter the ruins under moonlight, viewing every part with burning torchlights. The author and bookseller, Charles Heath, could barely keep pace with the demand for his *Historical and Descriptive Accounts of the Ancient and Present State of Tintern Abbey* (Monmouth 1793). By 1828 he had produced no fewer than eleven editions of this best-selling guide.

Burials in the Abbey Church

The Cistercians laid down strict regulations on burials within their abbey churches and cemeteries. Only highly significant patrons could expect to lie in the church, even if this rule was progressively relaxed in later centuries. At Tintern, both the first and the second abbey churches undoubtedly housed tombs of benefactors. Abbots may also have been buried in the church during the later Middle Ages.

Four members of the Marshal family were buried in the twelfth-century church: Isabel (d. 1220), Walter (d. 1245), Anselm (d. 1245), and Maud (d. 1248). A worn effigy of a knight in chain armour, dating from about 1240–50, may represent one of the Marshal brothers. Of further interest, in 1919–20 a grave was found in what is thought to have been the south transept of the early church. It probably represents Nicholas of Llandaff, treasurer of the cathedral there in 1196–1218. His tomb was hidden beneath the floor of the new church in the late thirteenth century.

As for the new church itself, tombstones recorded from the nave, south aisle, and south transept include those of Jenkyn ap Howell, William Vilemaydo (a one-time hermit given the title abbot), John Willifred, and William Wellsted. Moreover, there were at least two highly prestigious fifteenth-century burials in the church, recorded in both written descriptions and drawings. William Herbert, earl of Pembroke (d. 1469), and his wife, Anne (d. 1486), lay in a grand tomb chest before the high altar. North of this was the tomb of his son, William Herbert, earl of Huntingdon (d. 1490), and his wife, Mary Woodville (d. 1481).

Above: The brothers Walter and Anselm Marshal were both buried at Tintern in 1245. It is tempting to associate this mid-thirteenth-century tomb effigy at the site with one of the burials (© Crown copyright: Royal Commission on the Ancient and Historical Monuments of Wales).

William Herbert, earl of Pembroke, was buried in the abbey church in 1469. His wife Anne was buried with him in 1486. Their tomb was destroyed following the suppression of the abbey, though it was illustrated in the later family chronicle, the Herbertorum Prosapia *(Cardiff Central Library, Ms. 5.7).*

The west front of the abbey church in the later Victorian era. Although picturesque, the ivy had taken a fierce hold of the medieval stonework.

The Victorians and After

There was little sign of Tintern's 'Romantic' appeal waning as the nineteenth century progressed. A new road, unfortunately cutting through the medieval monastic precinct (p. 19), arrived in the early 1820s and brought with it a new generation of tourists. Writers of the time continued to heap praise on the beauty of the abbey church, but could scarce avoid mentioning the poorer homes of unfortunate local inhabitants. Like Gilpin and Coxe before them, the early Victorians were disturbed by the surrounding squalor. W. H. Thomas, for example, wrote in 1839 of his disappointment at seeing the abbey 'encumbered on every side with unpicturesque cottages and pigsties, rudely built with the consecrated stones of the violated ruin'.

By 1869 the approach to the church was said to be 'more pleasing' with the 'removal of several miserable hovels and pigsties', though it was thought more 'improvement' should follow. Sadly, however, not all actions in the Victorian era can now be considered improvements. In particular, the removal of the pulpitum (p. 44) was a great loss. It had survived the levelling works of the 1750s, and its base remained in position through to the second half of the nineteenth century, when it was captured in several early photographs. Its relevance to the ritual arrangements of the church had been lost, however, and its presence confounded those who wished for an uninterrupted vista along the full length of the building. The pulpitum was removed, without record, probably by about 1880.

The introduction of photography was to offer a new medium for recording charming views of the ivy-mantled ruins. And for the later Victorian tourist, with or without a camera, Tintern was to become yet more accessible with the completion of the Wye Valley Railway in 1876.

Later nineteenth-century scholars were to adopt a more enquiring approach to Gothic buildings. Across the country, ruined abbeys were to become the focus of more informed architectural and archaeological investigations. Tintern's significance had been highlighted as early as the 1840s through the appearance of two superb sets of drawings, the first by Joseph Potter (1847), to be followed by Edmund Sharpe (1848). In a pioneer study of the 1880s, Thomas Blashill went on to set out the foundations for our current understanding of the development of the abbey complex.

In 1901, Tintern was recognized as a monument of national importance. The abbey was purchased by the Crown from the ninth duke of Beaufort, via the Office of Woods, for the sum of £15,000. The ruins were in a fragile condition, and F. W. Waller (1846–1933), architect to Gloucester Cathedral, was engaged to supervise the necessary repair and maintenance. Works to the church were of paramount importance, but the domestic buildings around the cloister were also to receive attention.

With conservation progressing, in 1907 the Corsham architect and antiquary, Harold Brakspear (1870–1934), was commissioned to prepare a thorough ground plan of the abbey complex. He spent two weeks taking measurements on site, using a gang of labourers put at his disposal to 'excavate' in one or two places. His plan appeared in the first official guidebook, of which he was co-author.

In 1913–14, responsibility for Tintern passed to the Office of Works. At this time concern was mounting

Sir Harold Brakspear (1870–1934) made a ground plan of the abbey in 1907 and was co-author of the first official guidebook (The Brakspear family).

over the safety of the south nave arcade. It was thought to be in danger of imminent collapse, and timber shoring had been erected as an emergency measure. After much debate, major structural repairs were undertaken, beginning with the construction of a lattice girder roof over the south aisle. Then, in an enormous undertaking, with vast temporary brick supports, each of the piers of the arcade had to be dismantled. They were hollowed out to accommodate steel stanchions, which continue to support the weight of the wall above.

Gradually, the whole appearance of the abbey was transformed as the conservation programme moved steadily towards completion. The ivy, so beloved by the early tourists, but which caused so much decay to the stonework, had to be removed. Bit by bit, the post-monastic encroachments were cleared away, and more of the abbey buildings were uncovered and displayed. In August 1928, *The Daily Telegraph* could announce that the Tintern restoration scheme was practically complete.

Care and ongoing maintenance of the abbey have since been the responsibility of various government departments. In 1984, the duties passed to Cadw, which is now the historic environment service of the Welsh Assembly Government. A major fresh round of conservation was carried out on the church and some of the monastic buildings around 2000.

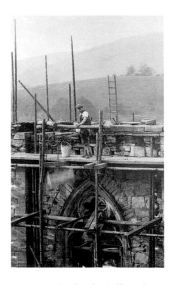

Conservation by the Office of Works in progress on the south wall top of the nave in May 1914.

Building the Abbey

Amid the daily round of worship at any large medieval monastic house, the monks must have grown accustomed to the habitual confusion of the building site. In this, Tintern was no exception. From what little we know of the abbey's archaeology below ground, and from the upstanding architecture in particular, it is clear that programmes of construction and rebuilding spanned the four centuries from the foundation to the suppression of the house. Few monks can have succeeded in spending their entire Cistercian lives free of the necessity of avoiding masons' scaffolding in one or other part of the abbey complex.

Early Buildings: Twelfth-Century

Building is likely to have begun even before the settling colony of monks arrived from l'Aumône in the spring of 1131. The founder, Walter of Clare, may have been responsible for providing a temporary arrangement of suitable structures. Guidance in this respect was laid down in one of the order's early regulations. Perhaps from as early as 1119, it was stipulated that no colony was to be sent out to a new location without the prior construction of such buildings as an oratory, a refectory, a dormitory, a guest chamber, and a porter's lodge or gatehouse. With these in place, judged the Cistercian fathers, the monks could 'immediately serve God and live in religious discipline'.

Generally, it seems such temporary structures were built of wood, though very little is known about their form or layout. At Tintern, as at other sites, we might imagine a modest timber church, together with associated domestic buildings, serving the pioneering community during its mission phase. As the abbey's position became secure, and with the community beginning to grow, the need for a permanent stone monastery would have become a priority.

Although few traces of the earliest masonry buildings can be readily identified above ground today, much can be gleaned from observations made during the conservation works in the early 1900s. In particular, a ground plan of the abbey church is recorded in outline. It was a cruciform (cross-shaped) building, with a small square-ended presbytery, and a narrow aisleless nave, measuring some 170 feet (52m) in total length. There were deep rectangular transepts to the north and south, each with two diminutive eastern chapels. From the design and scale of the plan, it might be suggested that the church was completed within about ten years of the foundation.

By the 1150s, work on the first stone cloister buildings was presumably also well advanced. Fragments of these survive encased within the walls of later phases of rebuilding, or now lie buried. Adjoining the north transept of the church, the east range was some 28 feet (8.5m) wide. On the ground floor, immediately next to the transept, it housed the chapter house (pp. 51–52). The northern part of the range may have served as part day room and part warming house. The whole of the first floor was occupied by the monks' dormitory. The refectory was situated in the adjacent north range, at this stage arranged on an east–west axis, parallel with the nave of the church.

Opposite: The presbytery of the abbey church, seen from the south transept. Begun in 1269, the Gothic building replaced a far more modest Romanesque structure of the community's pioneering years in the twelfth century.

In this early fourteenth-century manuscript illustration, a team of masons is seen completing work on a new church. Two black monks carry an altar, or perhaps a reliquary, in readiness for the consecration of the building (© The British Library Board, Royal Ms. 10 E. IV. f. 289v).

Suggested reconstruction of Tintern Abbey as it may have appeared at the end of the twelfth century. The drawing is based on little more than fragments of a ground plan, but it draws on knowledge of early Cistercian architecture elsewhere (Illustration by Terry Ball, 1990; with modifications, 1995, 2002).

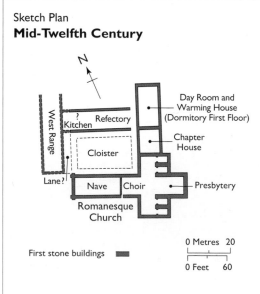

Sketch Plan
Mid-Twelfth Century

N

West Range

Kitchen
Refectory

Day Room and
Warming House
(Dormitory First Floor)

Cloister

Chapter
House

Lane?

Nave   Choir

Presbytery

Romanesque
Church

First stone buildings ▬

0 Metres 20
0 Feet   60

The range of buildings on the west side of the cloister would have been occupied by the lay brothers. It was often one of the earliest stone constructions at Cistercian abbeys. At Tintern, however, the twelfth-century arrangements are obscure. The plan may not have followed the common pattern, and the range may have been detached from the nave of the church. If this were the case, the cloister was probably separated from the lay brothers' accommodation beyond by a feature known as a 'lane'. Alternatively, the range could have been set out on a different alignment. This suggestion is supported by the angled footings of a twelfth-century doorway (p. 59) abandoned in a later phase of rebuilding.

Although relatively small, the proportions of the initial stone buildings at Tintern were comparable to those begun by other infant Cistercian communities before the mid-1140s. The church, for example, was of broadly similar proportions to that excavated at its sister abbey of Waverley, and there are suggestions of an even smaller aisleless church at Fountains in Yorkshire. However, we should remember that such simple layouts were not exclusive to the Cistercians in England and Wales at this time. Other communities seem to have been content with equally modest structures, notably within the broad congregation of Augustinian canons. Indeed, before the arrival of more standardized Cistercian planning a decade or so later, it is perfectly possible that blueprints for such forms could have come from outside sources.

But in any case, considering the general character of this first Tintern church, it is reasonable to assume that like many early Cistercian examples it had no crossing tower, and that the presbytery was roofed at a lower level than the nave. The walls would have been pierced by small round-headed windows, with colourless glass admitting clear light to the plain and simple proportions of the interior. The marginally thicker walls at the east end may have supported stone barrel vaults, both in the presbytery and the transepts, though the roof over the nave was probably of timber.

As a whole, Tintern's twelfth-century buildings doubtless conveyed an essential early Cistercian spirituality. This is something we can only really begin to appreciate in buildings of the next generation, as at Fontenay (Côte-d'Or) and Noirlac (Cher) in France, or Bonmont in Switzerland. Much closer, in south Wales, the austere beauty of the Romanesque Cistercian style can still be seen within the abbey church at Margam.

Rebuilding the Cloister Ranges: Late Twelfth to Mid-Thirteenth Century

New recruits were attracted to the noviciate at Tintern throughout the twelfth century, and before 1200 it was necessary to think about additional accommodation for the choir monks. Breaks in the side walls of the east range show that it was extended northwards by some 40 feet (12m), thereby providing for an increase in the size of the dormitory on the first floor.

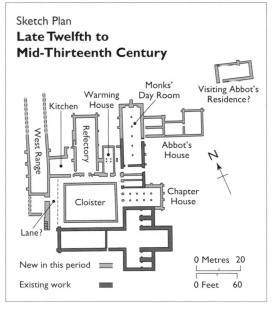

Sketch Plan
Late Twelfth to Mid-Thirteenth Century

New in this period
Existing work

0 Metres 20
0 Feet 60

The stripped austerity of the twelfth-century Romanesque nave at Margam Abbey (founded in 1147) testifies to the early Cistercian architectural ideal, and perhaps conveys something of the spirit of the initial stone buildings at Tintern.

A distinct break in the west side wall of the east range shows the position from which the block was extended in the late twelfth century.

A detail of one of the multi-clustered pier bases that supported the handsome archways leading into the remodelled thirteenth-century chapter house.

A wall capital and a section of the vault ribs in the warming house. This room was raised as part of the thirteenth-century remodelling of the north cloister range.

A latrine block, connecting with the dormitory, was set out alongside this new work.

Plans for a far more comprehensive reorganization of all three principal cloister ranges were to follow, with a major programme of construction extending through to the middle years of the thirteenth century. There is no clear record of the way the work progressed, though it should be noted that the 1224 grant from William Marshal the younger (p. 12) included the abbey's right to quarry building stone 'in the forest of Wyeswood'.

In the second half of the twelfth century, it had become customary Cistercian practice to build their refectories at right angles to the cloister, thereby creating additional space for chambers to the east and west. At Byland and Kirkstall in Yorkshire, the change may have taken place in the early 1170s, and before 1180 a similar pattern followed at neighbouring Fountains and Rievaulx, and again at Waverley in Surrey. At Tintern, although later, the thirteenth-century rebuilding was to include an arrangement on just these lines.

The new refectory was constructed from the north, which would have allowed the monks to use the earlier east–west structure for as long as possible. As the work advanced, a warming house was inserted in the space created to the east. The planning also made room for a day stair rising to the monks' dormitory in this north-east corner of the cloister. On the opposite side of the refectory, a kitchen was built where it could serve both the choir monks and the lay brothers (p. 58). When completed, the revised layout ensured that all the buildings essential to the monastic life were now directly accessible from the cloister.

In the meantime, the east range of cloister buildings had also undergone complete refurbishment. Here, the large buttresses built into the walls of the earlier northern extension *may* have anticipated the inclusion of a stone vault. In the thirteenth century, this was carried along the full length of the day room, with the ribs supported centrally by a row of five octagonal columns. On the ground floor, narrow lancet windows were fashioned in the side walls. Nothing survives of the dormitory arrangements above.

At the southern end of the east range, a bold new design for the thirteenth-century chapter house was in keeping with the importance of this room. First it was enlarged, with a free-standing eastern extension. Towards the cloister, three highly decorative archways created a striking entrance facade. Inside, below the floor of the dormitory, and in the extension to the east, stone vaults were inserted. These were supported on eight slender central columns, contributing to what must have been a very handsome and dignified chamber.

In all, from the detail seen in these works in the north and east ranges, it is tempting to associate some of the building progress with Abbot Ralph, from about 1232 until 1245 (p. 12). Even for a devout white monk, it seems the intoxicating beauty of the early Gothic architectural style had become too much to resist. Much of the work was unashamedly elaborate when compared to the simple purity of early Cistercian building. The master masons responsible appear to have been given free rein, producing playful variations of themes developed in a West Country school of architecture around the second quarter of the thirteenth century.

On the west side of the cloister, the range occupied by the lay brothers was also reconstructed by about 1250, or soon after. The northern half of the range scarcely survives above foundation level, making it difficult to resolve the full sequence of construction. To the north of the cloister, changes in the character of the masonry in both the east and west walls of this block reveal different building phases. South of these breaks, the ground floor was certainly vaulted in the thirteenth century. The outer parlour, at the southern end of the range, is of a similar date.

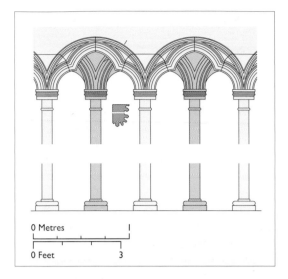

The Abbey Expands: Thirteenth Century

It is from the thirteenth century, too, that we can begin to trace the expansion of the abbey buildings beyond the immediate confines of the great cloister. There are two structures on the north-east side of the complex, which may well be broadly contemporary, and which appear to belong to the years before 1250.

The first of these lay immediately east of the monks' latrine, where an L-shaped chamber block survives, if heavily ruined. The building was probably linked with the latrine at first-floor level. It is likely to have served as accommodation for the abbot. Following the *Rule of St Benedict*, early Cistercian custom required the abbot to sleep in the common dormitory with his monks, though the duties required of his office made this increasingly difficult to maintain. Separate lodgings were becoming a necessity. At Tintern, as elsewhere, communication to the monks' dormitory, by way of the latrine, meant that the abbot could at least adhere to some semblance of the ideal.

As for the second building, again of two storeys, the surviving evidence suggests it would initially have been detached from the remainder of the monastery complex. Similarly positioned structures at other Cistercian sites have sometimes been interpreted as the lodgings provided for the abbey's visitor, in which case we might consider that the abbot of l'Aumône used this Tintern building on a number of occasions. Yet it is impossible to be certain, and other potential uses do present themselves. The block may, for example, have been connected with the earliest infirmary arrangements.

As it happens, the most significant addition to the monastic buildings in the second half of the thirteenth century was a large stone infirmary. Intended for the sick and aged monks, its location on the east side of the site conformed to general monastic planning. There may well have been other influences involved, but in this position the infirmary was at least isolated from the noise of the inner and outer courts. At Tintern, a vast aisled hall was raised, quite possibly replacing an earlier timber structure. With the completion of this new building, a second cloister enclosure had

With the completion of the cloister ranges, attention turned to the four alleys surrounding the central open court. Whatever the nature of the twelfth-century and interim arrangements, all was now to be laid out afresh. And, from investigations of loose stonework fragments at the site, we know that the arcades fronting the covered alleys were of fine craftsmanship. The design was based upon double rows of trefoil-headed arches set out in a staggered, or 'syncopated', pattern of considerable ingenuity. The work might well have been put in hand by about 1260, though clear differences in style may reflect several distinct stages of progress.

Above left: A reconstruction of two bays of the later thirteenth-century cloister arcade. The form of the arches varied around the garth (After Stuart Harrison).

Below left: The Tintern cloister arcade was of a similar general form to the 'syncopated' pattern surviving at the Benedictine abbey of Mont-St-Michel (Manche) in France (David Robinson).

In this manuscript illustration of about 1190–1200, a dying monk is shown on his sick bed within an abbey infirmary. The Tintern infirmary was first built in stone in the mid- to later thirteenth century (© The British Library Board, Additional Ms. 39943, f. 21).

Opposite: An impression of the new abbey church at Tintern under construction in the second half of the thirteenth century. Work began in 1269, with the building raised as a shell around the twelfth-century church. By 1288, the work was sufficiently advanced for the choir monks to take possession of the new east end. The old church had to be pulled down before the Gothic building could be completed, perhaps around 1300 (Illustration by Terry Ball, 1990; with modifications, 1995).

been created, again with an open central garth surrounded by arcaded alleys.

One other late thirteenth-century addition was the porch, built on to the outer parlour at the southern end of the west range. Its construction was probably related to a far more significant building programme then in hand.

A New Church: Late Thirteenth to Early Fourteenth Century

Having completed the various programmes of expansion on the claustral ranges, with very little pause the Tintern community embarked on the construction of a brand new abbey church. This long-delayed scheme would at last provide the monks with a true Gothic great church, one which would come to overwhelm the comparatively modest Romanesque structure of the pioneering years.

One near-contemporary chronicle records that the work was begun in 1269. A second chronicle, long since lost but known from an Elizabethan transcript, provides further evidence on the length of the building programme. For the year 1301, the chronicler recorded:

'*The new churche of Tintern Abbay, 32 yeres in building, was finished by Roger Bygod, and at his request was halowed the 5 kalends of August*'.

The beginnings of the scheme can therefore be traced to the time of Abbot John, who ruled the house between about 1267 and 1277. Roger Bigod's patronage can hardly be doubted, at least not during the later stages of construction. He was almost certainly present at the dedication ceremony in August 1301, and his generous gifts of 1301–02 may have provided the community with the essential finance to push through the final completion of the works. As noted above (pp. 14–15), however, it is rather more difficult to find explicit evidence for his involvement during the earliest years of the campaign. In any case, the liturgical furnishing and fitting out of the church were to continue for several decades after Roger's death in 1306.

The initial master mason appointed by Abbot John in 1269 was presented with the opportunity to build a new church from scratch, and in general terms the comprehensive unity of his original scheme is confirmed by an initial glance at the ruins. It is clear, however, that the builders were obliged to work within certain restrictions. The church had to be laid out slightly to the south of the twelfth-century edifice, with construction advancing in such a way that the monks might continue to use their earlier building for as long as possible. When the eastern part of the replacement church was sufficiently advanced, services could be transferred to the new choir and presbytery. In effect, the Gothic church grew as a shell around its smaller and much humbler predecessor.

Writing in the 1470s, William Worcestre informs us that enough progress had been made by Hock Day (15 April) 1287 to permit a Mass in the new church. Eighteen months later, on 3 October 1288, the choir monks were able to take possession of the presbytery with the first Mass celebrated at the high altar.

By this stage of building, if not earlier, it would have been necessary to dismantle the south transept of the older church, giving clear access to the newly consecrated choir and presbytery from the monks' dormitory to the north. In due course, as the masons resumed construction along the western bays of the nave, the remainder of the twelfth-century church would have been pulled down and its stone reused in the new works.

Sketch Plan
Late Thirteenth Century

Porch

Infirmary Cloister

Infirmary Hall

Romanesque Church

Choir — Presbytery

0 Metres 20
0 Feet 60

Gothic Church (under construction)   South Transept

New in this period
Existing work

N

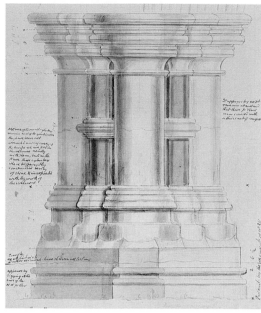

Over the three decades and more during which the programme was underway, variety began to creep into the initial design concept. Looking closely, there are clearly marked differences in the detail around the building. And, although not all of these can be used to chart the progress of the masons, several broad phases of construction can be identified. Whether more than one master mason was involved over the course of the works is a vexed question, as is the role — if any — of Master Ralph Gogun of London, known to have been employed by Roger Bigod at Chepstow Castle in the 1280s and early 1290s.

The windows are perhaps the most prominent features of the new church, with notable variation in the form of the tracery patterns from one section of the building to another. Even the method used by the glaziers to install the window glass altered as the work progressed. But there are other clues, too, which help us to fill out the construction story. In the presbytery and transepts, for example, each of the great clustered piers supporting the heavily moulded arches of the main arcades originally had four detached shafts in the angles. In the nave, on the other hand, all eight shafts in the piers were raised as coursed stonework, and here the arcade arches are of much less complex pattern.

At least one distinct break in the building programme seems to have occurred as the masons progressed westwards into the nave of the new church. The key to understanding this is in the detail around the southern windows, both in the aisles and in the clerestory. In particular, before the break, detached shafts were placed in the jambs at either side of the inner window edge. All of these have now disappeared. When work was resumed, the place of these shafts was taken by a roll moulding, which remains in position wherever it was used.

One of the last parts of the church to be completed was the section around the north transept. There was a complex constructional history in this area, with even a section of walling from the twelfth-century building retained within the fabric of the later masonry. The elaborate processional doorway into the church (p. 44), and the transept chapels and their windows belong to these later stages. Furnishing and fitting out the interior went on even longer. The elaborate pulpitum, for example, appears to have been installed within the nave around 1325–30 (p. 44). It is worth noting, too, that as late as 1340 there is a reference to 'the Keeper of the Work of the church of Tintern'.

As completed, the new church measured some 236 feet (72m) in overall length. Its ground plan was close in scale to that rebuilt in much the same period at the neighbouring Welsh house of Neath. Both churches reflect Cistercian preferences extending back to the late twelfth century, especially in the greatly extended presbytery, and (after about 1250) in the emphasis upon a large east window.

The overall impression is one of a building straddling the ideals of early Cistercian austerity and lavish cathedral splendour. The rather plain two-storey elevations in the nave and presbytery, the starkness of certain lines, and the effect of white limewash throughout are aspects which still seem to echo white monk ideals of earlier centuries. But no great church design of the later thirteenth century could ignore the influence of Westminster Abbey, rebuilt from 1245 by King Henry III (1216–72). In particular, this was the building which popularized the use of bar tracery in England. Thereafter, even for the Cistercians, the appearance of great church architecture was irreversibly transformed.

Tintern's greatest glory is its window tracery. The designs stem from impulses which spread throughout the country in the wake of Westminster. The vast eight light east window, for example, is much in the manner and scale of that in the Angel Choir at Lincoln Cathedral, begun in 1256. Yet the regional exemplar for such forms was perhaps the north transept at Hereford Cathedral, rebuilt about 1255–68. Indeed, it may well be that masons earlier employed at the cathedral were recruited for the work at Tintern. Whatever the case, by the time construction had progressed to the completion of the west front, new stylistic trends were in circulation. The seven-light window above the west door is no less impressive than its eastern counterpart, though its form seems to reflect a fresh generation of buildings from the last quarter of the century. Again it was London which led the way, and here the showcase in the 1270s and early 1280s was Old St Paul's Cathedral. The appearance of such a fashionable feature at Tintern could well reflect the influence of the well-travelled Abbot Ralph (p.15), the man who also negotiated with Roger Bigod over his patronage of the abbey.

Later Building: Fourteenth to Early Sixteenth Century

Another new architectural work associated with the final stages of the completion of the church was probably the now lost porch situated at the west front. All that remains are four hexagonal footings, which seem to date from the 1320s, and are assumed to represent an arcaded construction,

possibly associated with a small chapel (p. 40). By the early fifteenth century, 'the chapel without the west door of the church of the monastery of Tintern' housed a venerated statue of the Virgin Mary, and had become something of a pilgrimage centre.

All in all, although the final completion of the new church marked the end of a very definite stage in the development of the abbey complex, it was by no means the last significant building operation at Tintern.

Not least, as the position of the church now lay further south of the cloister garth, the southern alley and the adjacent arcades would have required modification and extension. From investigations of surviving loose stonework fragments, there is some

The patterns of bar tracery in the windows of the abbey church were perhaps its greatest glory. At the west end, the opening was filled with seven lights arranged in a two-three-two pattern. The tracery here reflects fashionable architectural developments of the late thirteenth century.

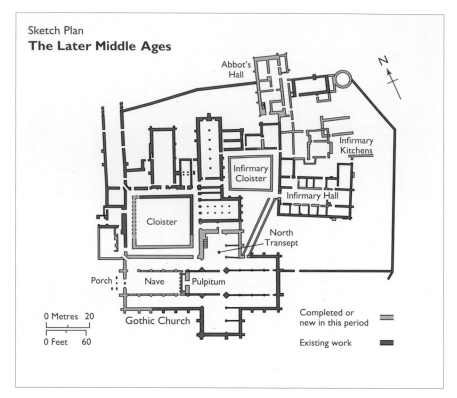

Sketch Plan
The Later Middle Ages

Abbot's Hall

N

Infirmary Kitchens

Infirmary Cloister

Infirmary Hall

Cloister

North Transept

Porch : Nave   Pulpitum

0 Metres 20

0 Feet   60

Gothic Church

Completed or new in this period ▬

Existing work ▬

A cast of the seal used by abbots of Tintern in the first half of the thirteenth century. A hand holds a pastoral staff, a symbol of the abbot's office. The Tintern abbots had separate quarters from the thirteenth century, but a grand new hall was built in the fourteenth century (National Museum of Wales).

evidence to support just such a restyling. At much the same time, a small courtyard was fashioned at the south end of the west range, adjoining an entry into one corner of the church.

However, the greatest undertaking of the fourteenth century was concerned with extensions and improvements to the abbot's residence (pp. 63–64). In particular, about 1330–45, an imposing new hall was built above a cellared undercroft on the north-east side of the site. The heads of Cistercian houses everywhere had become magnates of considerable local and even national importance. And the grand scale of the new hall at Tintern certainly reflects the status and aspirations of its abbots in the later Middle Ages. Apart from a lavish hall block, probably with direct access to the river frontage, additions were also made to the earlier thirteenth-century building in this area. A private chapel was housed in a two-storey extension to the south. A latrine, and even a dovecote, were added to the east.

From this enlarged and well-appointed abbot's complex, an ornate route led by way of the infirmary cloister towards the abbey church. The path was completed with a covered passage or gallery which also linked up with the infirmary hall.

The following century witnessed many minor alterations to existing abbey buildings. Although it is difficult to identify them precisely, we can be sure that private rooms for senior monks had become commonplace, and apartments are likely to have been provided for several of the corrodians, which the house found it necessary to support in the later Middle Ages.

A papal edict of 1335 gave the Cistercians limited permission to eat meat, and as the century progressed the practice increased. Meat dishes were supposed to be prepared in a separate kitchen and eaten in a distinct chamber, known as a misericord. The misericord was often located in the infirmary area of white monk monasteries. We cannot pinpoint such a building at Tintern, though one of the existing structures may well have been modified for the purpose.

Somewhat easier to identify are the changes which took place in the infirmary (pp. 60–62). Here, the aisles within the main hall had possibly been partitioned-off with wooden screens at an early date, but in the fifteenth century they were separated from the central nave of the building by solid stone walls. The aisles were divided into individual rooms, each with its own fireplace. The infirmary kitchen was also rebuilt and extended during the fifteenth century. By this time, however, it was serving a much wider role, not least in the provision of sumptuous dishes for the nearby abbot's hall.

Together these works reflect demands for increased comfort across the abbey complex. Significant changes had taken place within the Cistercian way of life, with much of the austerity of the early years long since gone. The lay brothers had ceased to be a major force, and servants had become an essential element in the daily life of the house. No longer was there a need for the great communal ranges of the cloister.

There are signs that early in the 1400s the monks began to consider that the open arcades of their cloister alleys had become outmoded. Subsequently, there were several attempts to improve the covered walks. In 1411–12, repairs were made to the existing roofs. Later in the century, a far more ambitious complete rebuilding was contemplated. The plan appears to have been to replace the draughty open arcades with a wall and glazed windows on the courtyard side. Indeed, in 1469, Earl William Herbert offered Tintern an endowment which included provision 'to build new cloisters'. Some progress was quite clearly made, with indications of its intended appearance in the south-east corner. The work was to be in Perpendicular style, and was to include a lavish stone-vaulted roof. But it seems the community was unable to complete the scheme.

In 1492, the abbey was pleading for finances to maintain its buildings. The pope granted a dispensation whereby the abbot was allowed to receive benefices to fund repairs to the monastery 'so threatened with ruin in its parts, walls, roofs, houses and granges and other buildings'. We can but guess at the reality of the situation. Finally, one of the last significant pieces of building we can readily identify is in the area above the warming house. Here, square-headed windows in late medieval style are the most prominent feature of a further chamber added over the lower two storeys on the very eve of the suppression.

An impression of Tintern Abbey towards the end of the Middle Ages. To the right, the infirmary and abbot's accommodation are shown with their later additions. To the top left, the form of the inner court buildings is far more conjectural (Illustration by Terry Ball, 1990; with modifications, 1995).

A Tour of the Abbey

The modern entrance to Tintern Abbey bears no relation to the monastic arrangements of the Middle Ages. To follow this tour, you should make your way across the site towards the west front of the church (see plan below). Here, you will stand close to the porch and outer parlour, through which privileged medieval visitors might have entered the heart of the abbey complex.

This tour begins with the abbey church itself, progressing along the nave to the choir, the presbytery, and the east end. From here the route moves out into the cloister garth and looks at each of the three main cloister ranges in turn. The description continues on the eastern side of the site, looking at the infirmary and related structures. The tour concludes with the abbot's hall and his associated private apartments.

Opposite: A view along the interior of the abbey church. The presbytery is in the foreground, and beyond lies the crossing and the nave, with the west door and window in the distance.

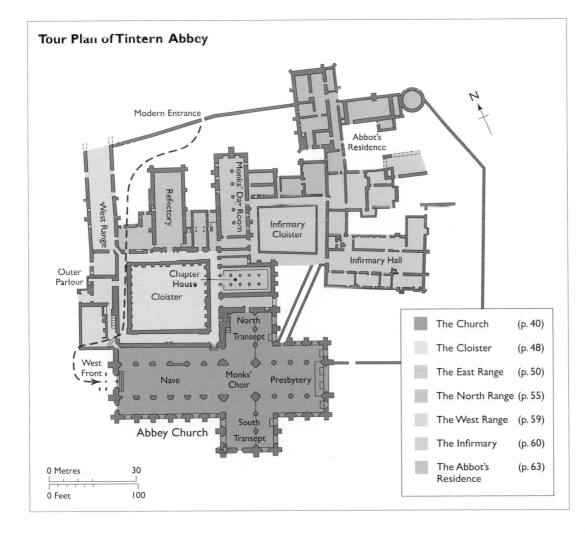

Tour Plan of Tintern Abbey

Modern Entrance

Abbot's Residence

Monks' Day Room

Refectory

West Range

Infirmary Cloister

Infirmary Hall

Outer Parlour

Chapter House

Cloister

North Transept

West Front

Nave

Monks' Choir

Presbytery

South Transept

Abbey Church

0 Metres 30
0 Feet 100

■	The Church	(p. 40)
■	The Cloister	(p. 48)
■	The East Range	(p. 50)
■	The North Range	(p. 55)
■	The West Range	(p. 59)
■	The Infirmary	(p. 60)
■	The Abbot's Residence	(p. 63)

These fragments of a fine thirteenth-century statue of the Virgin and Child, found at Tintern, have been reassembled outside the visitor centre. This figure is a reminder that all white monk abbeys were dedicated to St Mary the Virgin.

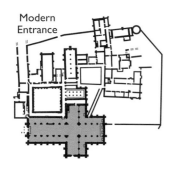

Modern
Entrance

The Church

The West Front

Completed within a few years of 1300, the west front of Tintern's grand Gothic church remains its most endearing feature. At first glance, it works very well as an architectural whole. When we begin to study the various elements in detail, however, several distinct stylistic differences begin to emerge. In particular, the huge central window almost certainly represents a later phase of construction than some of the lower areas. Note, too, the very clear disparity between the form of the windows in the two side aisles.

The central doorway features two trefoil-headed openings, above which paired sub-arches sit within the main enclosing arch. Between these is an almond-shaped niche known as a vesica, which probably housed a statue of the Virgin and Child. Some of the surrounding panel work is decorated with pretty diaper carving, although this may never have been fully completed. To the sides of the doorway, the paired niches set within blind tracery arcading were doubtless intended for statues of saints. On the far right, a secondary doorway opens into the south aisle.

Towering over the central doorway, the great west window is of seven lights arranged in a two-three-two pattern. Recently restored, virtually all of its tracery remains intact. The pointed 'trilobe' and 'dagger'

patterns in the head represent fine examples of the late thirteenth-century Decorated style.

The column bases in front of the west door are the only remains of a porch added here in about 1320–30. It has been suggested that this arcaded construction also supported the chapel housing a revered statue of Our Lady (p. 17). Such an elevated building would have partially blocked the lower sections of the west window, and it is worth noting an alternate possibility. Around to the right, beyond the corner buttresses, in 1904–05 foundations thought to represent a 'small chapel' were revealed along the side of the south aisle.

For the monks themselves, the importance of this grand west front lay in ritual and display, and in ceremony. In particular, the porch and central doorway served as an entrance for major feast-day processions. Our own perceptions of the drama involved are further heightened when we appreciate that the whole facade was probably painted.

The Nave

You should now move through the west door into the abbey church proper. Built to replace a much smaller twelfth-century edifice, this was the church begun — according to the abbey's lost chronicle — in 1269. The difference in scale and position between the two buildings is best appreciated by observing and pacing out the southern foundations of the first church. The alignment of its walls is marked in outline on the present ground surface. A grille is situated at the south-west corner, with the plinth of a Romanesque pilaster buttress surviving below. Around these fragmentary traces, the later Gothic church remains remarkably complete.

The nave itself is divided into six bays, defined as the spaces between the pairs of columns or piers arranged along the length of the building. The central area was divided from aisles to the north and south by arcades of pointed arches. These sprang from moulded capitals set on the sturdy clustered piers, each comprising eight rounded shafts. The piers were in turn linked by solid screen walls some 11 feet (3.4m) high. The stubs of these walls still remain in position. Over the arcade, the middle stage of the nave elevation — the triforium — was plain. And above this were the

Opposite: The west front of the abbey church. The vast seven-light window is a good example of the contemporary Decorated style, strongly influenced by late thirteenth-century developments in London.

Below: This drawing of the west door was made by W. J. Allen in 1870. Allen shows the various details, including the fine diaper work, as originally designed. In the vesica above the door, he shows a statue of the Virgin and Child.

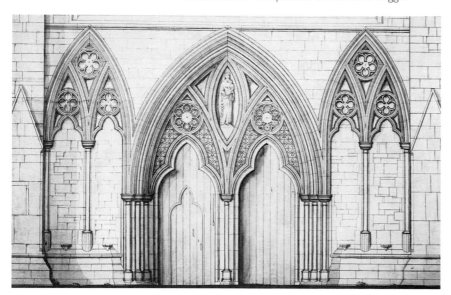

The contrasting window styles in the western bays in the south aisle of the nave.

The vault shafts in the south wall of the nave spring from decorative corbels. This example depicts two beasts fighting.

A fragment of wall plaster in the north transept. Imitation masonry joints are picked out as red lines.

clerestory windows, each of two lights with six-lobed cusped heads.

The north arcade had collapsed before the early eighteenth century, and its southern counterpart was just saved from a similar fate by a system of steel reinforcing (p. 25). This work was undertaken between 1913 and 1924, at which time a new roof was placed over the south aisle, since replaced.

As designed, the western bays of the nave were intended for the abbey's lay brothers. Although they were illiterate men, the *conversi* did take religious vows and wore the habit, attending mainly night offices in this part of the church. An entrance leading from their quarters in the west cloister range was set diagonally in the far north-west corner. From here, a break in the first bay of the northern screen wall would have given access to their central choir. We might envisage their choir stalls backing on to the partition walls in the second and third bays of the nave.

In Cistercian churches of the twelfth and thirteenth centuries, the lay brothers' choir was

The Internal Appearance of the Abbey Church

The open space encountered in the abbey church today is deceptive. When completed, the building was divided up by screen walls and partitions to suit contemporary Cistercian liturgical and ritual arrangements.

As designed, the church was never meant to be seen or used as a whole. Solid stone screen walls ran between the two rows of arcade piers along the entire length of the building. These walls divided the central part of the church from an aisle at either side. In turn, this centrally screened section was divided across its width by at least two further stone partition walls. One of these, the pulpitum, was particularly elaborate (p. 44). In this way several distinct areas were created for specific allocation and functions.

Very little of the local red-green sandstone (quarried on nearby Barbadoes Hill) would have been left exposed. The church would have had an altogether brighter appearance, conveying the importance of living light within Cistercian architecture. A few surviving fragments tell us that the wall faces were white lime plastered, with lines depicting imitation stonework joints picked out in red. By the end of the Middle Ages, it is possible

that scenes of greater elaboration were painted in chapel spaces or prominent positions.

The brightness of the walls was complemented by the sheen from the floor of the church. Large areas were paved with richly decorated and glazed tile pavements. The primarily red-brown clay tiles carried heraldic, symmetrical, and naturalistic designs picked out in white pipeclay. More than thirty separate designs are known from Tintern. The tiles would have been combined in patterned groups, almost certainly in the presbytery, the choir and transepts.

Overhead, the entire church was covered by stone vaults. In the nave and presbytery, in the spaces between the arches of the arcades (spandrels), triple shafts are carried on carved corbels. The shafts in turn support the splayed 'springers', which took the weight of the vault ribs. The ribs ran out in transverse and diagonal lines, creating a simple quadripartite (four part) pattern. There were large bosses at the intersections of the diagonal ribs, examples of which can be seen in the south nave aisle. The whole was almost certainly painted, particularly the leaf-like designs of the bosses.

closed off from the area to the east by the rood screen; the screen taking its name from an image of Christ on the cross which it supported. The bay beyond the rood served as the retrochoir, the place in the church where infirm and aged monks were allowed to sit during the offices. Beyond this, another more elaborate screen, the pulpitum, generally crossed the nave between the next pair of piers.

At Tintern, it is far from clear what survived of such traditional arrangements when the handsome stone pulpitum (p. 44) was built between the fifth pair of nave piers, probably about 1325–30. Apart from a solid stone wall linking the piers, the pulpitum included a five-bay vaulted projection, fronted by an elaborate arcade extending westwards. It may well be that by the mid-fourteenth century, the great rood was positioned above this same screen.

Retracing our steps a little, we must bear in mind that the nave aisles were initially designed as passages linking the two ends of the church. Cut off as they were from the central part of the nave, both aisles

were lit by windows in each of the bays. These were of varying design. In the south aisle, the windows in the four bays to the east were similar to those in the clerestory: two lights with six-lobed cusped heads. The windows in the two western bays were somewhat different. Again they were of two lights, but they were much smaller, with higher sills, and this time with four lobes to the cusping of the head. In part, these stylistic changes probably reflect different phases in the construction of the church.

Cutaway reconstruction of the abbey church showing the internal liturgical arrangements and decoration about 1330. The form of the flèche over the crossing, and of the porch outside the west door are somewhat conjectural (Illustration by Terry Ball, 1995; with modifications, 2002).

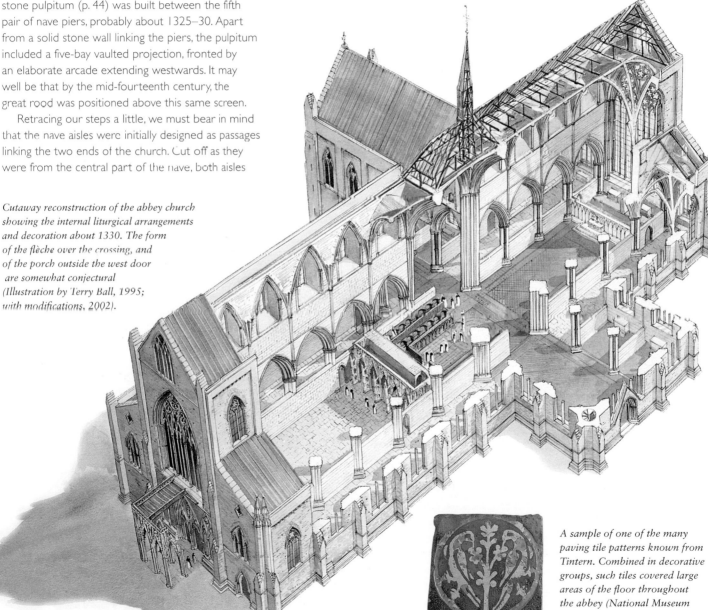

A sample of one of the many paving tile patterns known from Tintern. Combined in decorative groups, such tiles covered large areas of the floor throughout the abbey (National Museum of Wales).

The Pulpitum

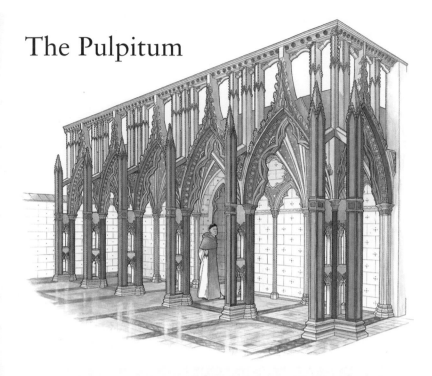

A reconstruction of the Tintern pulpitum, which is dated to about 1325–30. The colour scheme is conjectural (After Harrison, Morris and Robinson 1998; drawing by Chris Jones-Jenkins, 1998; with modifications, 2010).

Fragments of the blind tracery from the back wall of the pulpitum.

Despite strong elements of Cistercian restraint seen in Tintern's second church, the pulpitum represents an unexpected burst of highly decorative architecture. A solid screen wall ran between two of the nave piers and supported an elaborate arcade facing west. Five ogee-headed arches spanned the width of the nave. Each was richly decorated with ball-flowers and naturalistic foliage; the whole surmounted with an embossed cornice standing up to 18 feet (5.5m) high.

The discovery of such a glamorous liturgical fitting within a Cistercian context is particularly rare, though a similar example at Exeter Cathedral serves to remind us that such screens appear to have come into fashion in the early fourteenth century. Probably installed in the late 1320s, the Tintern screen was of the very highest quality.

The stylistic context for the work lies largely within the great architectural lodges of south-west England, places such as Bristol, Exeter and Wells. There are strong grounds for suggesting that its designer was the innovative West Country mason, Master William Joy.

In the north aisle, the windows belong to the later phase of building. They are once more of two lights, with far higher sills. Here, however, the high sills would have been necessary to clear the roof of the covered cloister walk outside (pp. 48–49).

The bay at the east end of the north aisle belongs to the final stages in the construction of the church. The window tracery was richer, and below is the processional doorway through which the choir monks entered the church from the cloister for services during the day. This is best appreciated by stepping outside. Note the sumptuous carving of the head, together with the rich surrounding mouldings and frilly decorative detail. There is a large panel with a pointed trilobe above.

Before we leave the nave, it is somewhat ironic to consider that its construction coincided with the gradual demise of the lay brothers as a significant force at Tintern. By the middle years of the fourteenth century, their special allocation within the church was no longer required. In the absence of firm archaeological evidence, we can but surmise as to the subsequent use of the nave. It seems likely that it was only used regularly for ceremonial purposes, with the elaborate pulpitum forming the climax to the vista from the west door, and from various processional stations along the nave.

As at other Cistercian houses, some of the bays in the north and south aisles were probably converted to chapels, with the screen walls removed to provide access. This would have facilitated the increasingly usual practice in the later Middle Ages of each priest-monk offering a daily Mass. In addition, such chapels may have constituted chantries and may have housed the tombs of benefactors.

The Monks' Choir and Presbytery

From the bay immediately beyond the pulpitum, almost to the far east end of the church, the centrally screened-off area was occupied by the monks' choir and presbytery. By virtue of the surrounding screen walls, it may be thought of as a church set within the abbey church as a whole. The monks gained access either from the west, through the door at the centre of the pulpitum, or through a break in the screen wall facing the north transept. It was here that the late thirteenth-century masons had concentrated their efforts. Compared with the nave, the richness of the moulding in the arches of the arcades, for example, or the once detached shafts in the angles of the piers represent rather more elaborate forms of contemporary architectural detailing.

The choir itself extended from the last bay of the nave into the area between the four great cross-arms of the church. The monks' stalls, probably of richly carved oak, backed on to the pulpitum, and against the screen walls to the sides. You will see that the clusters of shafts on the inner faces of the two western crossing piers are not carried all the way to the ground. This arrangement was intended to accommodate the backs of the choir stalls.

The choir was at the very heart of what St Benedict had called the *opus Dei* (the work of God) — the fundamental framework for the monastic day. From Benedict's *Rule*, the Cistercians followed the example of the Old Testament prophet, singing the praises of God seven times a day, and at night rising to confess him. This meant a long round of eight divine offices in the choir. Everything else was determined by this routine, day in and day out. Within the earlier abbey church, one generation of Tintern monks seems to have been a little too enthusiastic in its daily round. In 1217 the order's General Chapter rebuked them for singing their office in harmony, 'in the manner of seculars'.

The area at the centre of the church is known as the crossing. This is the space between the nave and presbytery, and between the north and south transepts. The crossing is surrounded by four great arches, rising from massive multi-clustered piers. High in the corners, there are traces of the stone vault which sprang overhead. Above this, the roofs of the church appear to have met without a central crossing tower, in the manner of many contemporary French Gothic churches. The crossing point may well have been crowned with an octagonal spired flèche, large enough to have housed bells. William Worcestre noted a 'belfry' over the choir in the fifteenth century; and, at the suppression, the abbey's four bells, weighing 21 hundredweight (1,067kg), were estimated to value £10.

The presbytery occupied the three bays from the crossing towards the east end of the church. It was approached via at least one step up from

A manuscript illustration of 1268 showing two scenes from a Cistercian abbey church. At the bottom, a group of monks sing loud and clear in the choir. At the top, a monk is shown celebrating Mass at the high altar (Stiftsbibliothek Zwettl, MS. 400, f. 1v).

Below: The presbytery looking towards the great east window, with the south transept arcade to the right.

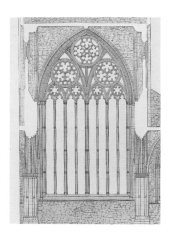

A reconstruction of the tracery in the east window of the abbey church. It was filled with stained glass, some bearing the arms of Roger Bigod. This detail is taken from Edmund Sharpe's Architectural Parallels *(London 1848), plate B. 52.*

Above: The blocked archway below the great east window may have been used as a barrow way during the construction of the church.

A view from the north transept looking south and east. Notice the elevation in the foreground, where the need to accommodate wall-passages led the master mason to create the impression of a third storey.

the choir. Although richer in detail, the elevation of the arcades is similar to that in the nave. The piers were again linked by partition walls, but here they are thinner and lower. The blank triforium level is marked by projecting stringcourses, and the clerestory windows have the usual two lights above the level of the aisle roofs.

The high altar was situated in the third bay, in front of a further parclose or screen wall across the church. Towering above, separated by a single bay, was the huge eight-light east window. Apart from the great central mullion, formed from a cluster of shafts (replaced in 1904–05), it has lost most of its stone tracery. However, William Worcestre tells us it was 'glazed with the arms of Roger Bigod the Founder'.

The Eastern Aisles

The north, south and east aisles in this part of the church were cut off from the presbytery by the screen walls. They served as a processional walk, part of the route between the north and south

transepts. Four lesser altars were positioned against the eastern wall, two behind the high altar on a raised platform which is still in position, and one in each aisle. Breaks or arches in the north and south screens of the last bay would have allowed for the passage of processions. There were three-light windows above the aisle altars, and a two-light window in each of the side bays.

In the last bay of the south aisle, the recess in the outer wall may have contained a piscina, or small basin used to cleanse the sacramental vessels. In the middle of the east wall, below the great window, notice the low blocked arch. It may indicate a barrow way used by the builders during the construction of the church. Finally, at the western end of the north aisle, there is a doorway which gave access to the passage leading towards the infirmary. This covered gallery also provided an ornate route by which later medieval abbots and their guests might enter the church.

The Transepts

The two large cross-arms of the church were formed by the north and south transepts. Both transepts are of broadly similar design, with the detailing echoing that in the presbytery. The main walls rise to the full height of the church, but each has a lower eastern aisle divided into chapels. The most significant difference from the remainder of the church is in the elevations. The need to accommodate wall-passages, allowing access to roof spaces, led the builders to create big open arches to the back of the clerestory windows. This occurs on both sides of the north transept, and in the west wall of the south transept. The design seems to imply a third storey, without there actually being one.

In the south transept, the end wall is pierced by a very tall window, originally of six lights, though its tracery has all been lost. There is a doorway beneath, with its bold triangular gable extending into the lower part of the window. This doorway was used for processional purposes, and probably gave access to the monks' cemetery to the east of the church. A circular stairway in the south-west angle led to the gallery passage in the west wall, and then on to the roof space over the south aisle of the nave.

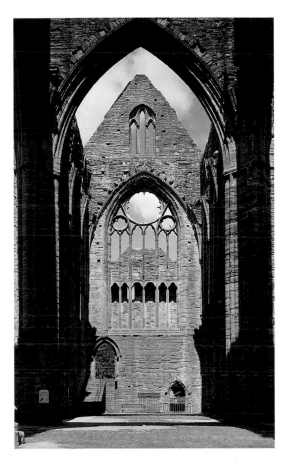

The eastern arcade led into two chapels, separated from each other, and from the presbytery aisle, by screen walls. You will see the base of an altar surviving in the northern chapel. Both chapels had three-light windows above the altars.

The constructional history of the north transept was complex, owing to the fact that the east end of the first church lay in this area. The end wall was again pierced by a large six-light window, retaining much of its stone tracery, though here the moulded detailing was handled differently from that in the great east and south windows. Also, you will see that the glass was never carried all the way down, with the lower part of the tracery treated as panelling. Outside, the roof of the monks' dormitory butted against the wall of the transept at this point.

In the north-west corner was the night stair. The existing steps date from 1905, but they are built on the line of the originals and lead to a doorway through which the monks entered the church from their dormitory for services during the hours of darkness. Also in this corner, there is a circular stair leading from dormitory level to the wall gallery, and to the outer roof of the church.

To the right of the night stairs, a doorway at ground level gave access to the sacristy or vestry (p. 50). The eastern chapels were again divided from one another by screen walls. The base of an altar can be seen in the northern chapel. Some of the plaster which covered the walls of the church also survives in this area. The fragments of tracery in the east chapel windows reveal that this was one of the last areas of the church to be completed. Above the chapels, there are the abutments for two flying buttresses, a feature that does not occur elsewhere at Tintern.

Above: A reconstruction of the north transept with the monks descending the night stair for a service in their choir during the hours of darkness. The low doorway to the right led into the sacristy. The blocked area of window below the tracery head marks the gable of the monks' dormitory outside (Illustration by Terry Ball, 1995).

Above left: The north transept was the last area of Tintern's Gothic church to be completed in the early fourteenth century.

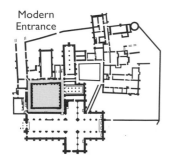

Modern
Entrance

The Cloister

At the centre of the cloister was an open court, or garth. It was enclosed by four covered passages, or alleys, now marked by broad gravel paths. This view looks north-east across the cloister. The low walls at the edge of the now grass-covered garth mark the position of the surrounding arcades.

When not at the work of God in the abbey church, the monks spent much of their time in the great cloister. It comprised a large open court or garden, known as the cloister garth, surrounded on each of the four sides by broad covered passages, or alleys. The alleys themselves provided living space for the community. This was where the choir monks read, studied, and meditated; it may also have been where they washed and did their laundry. At Tintern, somewhat unusually, the cloister was built to the north of the church. Otherwise, the arrangements of the surrounding buildings conform to the broad Cistercian plan.

Initially, a cloister would have been set out to accompany the first abbey church. But in the mid- to later thirteenth century, following a major remodelling of the monastic buildings, the entire cloister was reconstructed. In this phase, the alleys were designed with open arcades of the most striking beauty and originality. The garden was enclosed with two rows of columns, arranged in a staggered or 'syncopated' pattern, and supporting trefoil-head arches. Despite the quality of the workmanship, however, such open arcades left the alleys exposed to the elements. Life within was doubtless cold and cheerless in winter.

In the mid- to late fifteenth century, the monks decided it was once again time to bring their cloister alleys up to date. We cannot be certain of the extent of progress made at this time, but there are clear indications of the planning. The most obvious signs are the thickened wall foundations you will see to the edge of the present gravelled surfaces. The bases of an irregular series of projecting buttresses also belong to the fifteenth-century scheme. Moreover, in the south-east corner of the garth, there are traces

of carved stone panelling. The intention appears to have been to enclose the alleys with walls and vaulted roofs. Windows would have provided the necessary light and comfort.

A large number of corbels which carried the earlier lean-to roofs can be seen in the walls around the cloister alleys. On the south and west sides, in particular, these are set at two distinct levels. In the centre of the cloister, the present grass cover is deceptive. In the monastic centuries, it is likely to have been a true garden, with flowers, herbs, and perhaps even fruit trees.

In monastic cloisters generally, the alley against the church was that used by the monks for reading and study. At Tintern, the fifteenth-century remodelling would not have overlooked the need to accommodate desks, or carrels in this area. In this same alley, there is evidence of a somewhat rare Cistercian feature associated with periods of study. Low in the centre of the church wall, and set into the stone bench which runs along the full length of the alley, you will see the remains of a canopied seat. This was where the abbot sat to listen during *Collation*, a name derived from the *Collationes* of St John Cassian (d. about 435), one of the books recommended for reading. Afterwards, the monks proceeded into the choir for the final evening service of *Compline*.

A reconstruction of the cloister garth and surrounding arcades as they may have appeared towards the end of the thirteenth century. The view looks into the north alley and shows the lavatorium *where the monks washed in ritual fashion before meals (Illustration by Terry Ball, 1990; with modifications, 1995).*

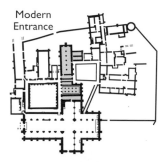

In the twelfth century, two round-headed cupboards set into the wall of the church served to hold books read by the monks in the north cloister alley. One of the cupboards was later blocked.

The East Range

You should now turn to look at the east range where this tour of the buildings around the great cloister begins. Adjoining the north transept, the range runs out beyond the cloister proper and has an overall length of some 170 feet (52m). It was reserved almost exclusively for the use of the choir monks.

Book Room and Sacristy

Before proceeding to the individual chambers of the range, it is worth noting the two round-headed recesses in the face of the north transept wall. One of these remains open, but the second was blocked during the fifteenth-century cloister modifications. These recesses began life as book cupboards, built as they were into the north transept of the twelfth-century church.

In fact, the first of the east range rooms, adjoining the later church, was a more spacious book store (the *armarium*). It was entered through a doorway with deeply moulded splays, a central trumeau and traceried head, the details of which suggest a date of about 1300. The space inside now looks like one long chamber, though originally it was divided into two rooms by a solid wall. In the book store to the front, there are traces of a plain barrel vault.

The room to the rear could be entered from the north transept of the church. This was the vestry (*vestiarium*) or sacristy, the place where the vestments and liturgical vessels used in Masses and other services were stored in safety. Part of the three-bay vaulted roof survives, and there is a large aumbry or cupboard in the south wall. We know that the floor was tiled. Above this room, a door led from the southern end of the monks' dormitory into a strong room or treasury which was also in the charge of the sacrist.

In the 1530s Tintern still possessed, among other such items, a fine crozier, four chalices and patens, two wooden crosses plated with silver gilt and jewels, two candlesticks, and two censers with an incense boat. The abbey was also spending up to £8 a year on bread and wine, and on wax and oil to light the church. Much would have been stored either in the sacristy or the room above.

The Tintern Bible

A thirteenth-century Bible, identified as belonging to the Tintern library (National Library of Wales, Ms. 22631 C).

All medieval monastic houses built up collections of books. In this, the Cistercians were no exception. The Yorkshire abbey of Rievaulx, for example, is identified as having 212 volumes in the thirteenth century, and Flaxley in Gloucestershire had seventy-nine. The importance of books was reflected in the statutes of the order, and periods of two to four hours a day were set aside for reading. We can be sure that Tintern amassed a library of its own. There are two early book cupboards in the east cloister walk, and there is an adjacent library room, the *armarium*. But only one surviving volume can now be specifically assigned to Tintern, namely a thirteenth-century Bible.

The Chapter House

North of the book store and vestry was the chapter house, a large and once splendid chamber of very great importance. The monks assembled here each morning, sitting on the stone benching around the outer walls whilst the abbot or his deputy presided over the chapter meeting. The proceedings began with the reading of a lesson. A chapter from the *Rule of St Benedict* was then read out, whence the name of the room is derived. Saints and benefactors were commemorated, and on certain feast days the abbot might deliver a sermon. It was here, too, that faults were confessed, accusations made, and penances assigned. The meeting would then move on to discussions of abbey business and administration. In sum, the chapter house should be seen as the primary gathering place for the community.

The chapter house was entered from the cloister by way of a quite stunning group of three richly clustered arches, an arrangement of considerable originality. Little now remains, though the bases of the two central piers reveal something of the sumptuous quality. They were composed of clusters of no less than fourteen shafts, six of which were coursed and eight detached. Inside, the rectangular space was broken by eight elegant columns supporting the rib-vaulted roof. The columns divided the room into three bays across its width, and five bays along its length.

The three western bays lay under the floor of the monks' dormitory, and so the vault had to be contained beneath the level of this upper floor. By the later Middle Ages, if not earlier, these bays would have served merely as a vestibule. The chapter house proper was contained within the two free-standing eastern bays, which were of yet more imposing design. They lay outside the width of the range and therefore allowed for a higher vault. These bays were also longer, confirming that this eastern area was an extension to the original chapter house plan.

The room was lit by a series of tall windows, all of which were situated in the east bays. There seem to have been three sets of triple-light openings along the end wall, and there were further windows in the adjacent side bays. The opening in the south-east bay was blocked with the construction of the sacristy in the early fourteenth century.

Traces of the stone benches on which the monks sat can still be seen, raised on a platform along the

This fine doorway of about 1300 led from the east cloister alley into the abbey's book room.

Although the chapter house does not survive to any great height, it was clearly a once splendid chamber and was of very great importance as the principal gathering place for abbey meetings.

A reconstruction of the choir monks attending their daily meeting within the chapter house. Much of the detail is based on firm archaeological and architectural evidence (Illustration by Terry Ball, 2002).

Right: The round-headed window at the northern end of the monks' day room belongs to a late twelfth-century extension of the range.

Opposite: The monks' day room, looking south towards the north transept of the abbey church. The octagonal columns supported a stone vault inserted in the thirteenth century. Notice the crease of the dormitory roof against the church.

monks' dormitory (p. 54). These may have been of wood; certainly nothing survives, and the space may later have served as a passage.

North of this once more, a wider passage led through the range, linking the cloister to the infirmary buildings. From this, a door in the north wall leads into the monks' day room.

The Monks' Day Room

The *Rule of St Benedict* required that part of the monk's day should be spent at work, and for the early Cistercians this was to be taken literally. The brothers undertook a variety of appropriate tasks within the day room, the long chamber on the ground floor at the northern end of the east range. For part of the abbey's history, the novices may also have been accommodated in this room. As completed in the first half of the thirteenth century, it was a fine hall covered with a stone vault in six bays. The vault ribs were supported on a central row of five octagonal piers, and on corbels with moulded capitals set into the side walls.

The first three bays represent the original twelfth-century chamber. The room was enlarged, probably no later than about 1200, with a round-headed window of this phase surviving in the far right-hand corner. Before the comprehensive rebuilding of the cloister ranges, an area at the southern end of this long chamber may have served as the warming house (pp. 55–56). You will see traces of a fireplace, with a 'herringbone' pattern of masonry along its rear

sides of the room. The floor was covered with a decorative tile pavement, with some of the smaller border tiles remaining in place.

In common with the normal monastic practice, the Cistercians used the chapter house as a burial space for deceased abbots. At Tintern, at least one grave was discovered in the floor of the chamber in the early twentieth century. In the cloister alley outside, five grave slabs can still be seen, but all have lost their inscriptions.

Parlour and Passage

Next to the chapter house, another doorway with jambs of clustered shafts led into the parlour. Traditionally, this is seen as the place where the monks were allowed to talk on important matters without breaking the cloister rule of silence. Yet its primary purpose may have been to serve as an office for the prior. Here at Tintern, the room was presumably stone vaulted, so as to support the thrust from the vault in the adjacent chapter house. It was lit by a single window at the east end.

The narrow space north of the parlour probably contained the original day stairs down from the

A detail of the abbey drain which ran below the floor at the northern end of the monks' day room.

face, sitting below one of the two later lancet windows in the east wall.

The vault was inserted as part of the remodelling of the range in the first half of the thirteenth century. The narrow lancet windows, with their deep rear splays, also belong to this phase. As a whole, however, the rather poor provision of window openings must have left the room somewhat dark. Natural daylight was probably supplemented with lamps hung from the vault ribs.

At the northern end of the day room, certain details of the main abbey drain can be observed. Within the now open channel, sharply grooved stones at each side mark the position of sluice gates. The water level could be raised before it was released through to the adjoining monks' latrine. Raising the water level also released water through a higher, secondary, channel running north-east towards the abbot's complex (pp. 63–64). The water supply to these drains was always of great importance. By 1528, the abbot had to prevent anyone 'washing any dirty thing, clothes or other corrupt matter, in the stream which runs through the middle of the abbey', under penalty of a 7s. fine.

The Monks' Dormitory

Although few of its details have survived, almost the entire upper floor of the east range was occupied by the monks' dormitory. Looking south from the day room, high up against the north transept of the church, you will see the pitch of its gabled roof crease. Of course, the alignment reflects the relationship of the dormitory to the original twelfth-century church. It is overlapped by the wider transept of the later building.

If the internal arrangements followed early Cistercian custom, the monks' beds would have been arranged along the walls, with clothes presses filling the centre of the room. Beds of wood were probably lined with straw, and were covered with canvas mattresses which were themselves filled with straw. In this confined, and at times warm and dusty environment, the brothers were expected to sleep fully clothed in their habits.

For the newly professed monk, entering the dormitory for the first time, and looking along the two rows of beds stretched out for some 170 feet (52m), the prospect of his first few nights' sleep must have seemed daunting. The

scale of this great chamber suggests it might easily have accommodated anything up to eighty or even a hundred brothers. In the later Middle Ages, however, with fewer monks, and with demands for greater privacy and comfort, the room was probably partitioned with curtains or wooden screens into a number of individual cells.

The Latrine

Projecting eastwards at right angles to the day room is the latrine block. It was a two-storey building, divided into northern and southern halves by a partition wall. From the dormitory, the monks would have gained direct access to a row of first-floor privies situated to the north of the cross-wall. These privies stood on timber flooring and were arranged over the drainage sewer which ran below.

The ground-floor room in the southern half of the block had a stone-vaulted roof. It was fitted with a door and windows facing the infirmary cloister. At the west end of the cross-wall, there was a latrine with its chute discharging into the main drain.

Although it has been suggested that part of the monks' day room may have been set aside as accommodation for the novices (p. 52), a case could also be made for this southern chamber within the latrine block. Situated outside the world of the cloister proper, it was close enough to allow the novices some contact with the more experienced professed monks.

Right: The foundations of the monks' latrine block. The privies were situated above the drainage sewer which can be seen at the bottom right of this view.

The North Range

Returning to the cloister, we may turn next to look at the details of the north range. This took its present form in the first half of the thirteenth century, with the eastern part still surviving to second-floor level.

Day Stair

You should begin at the large, recessed archway at the east end. This of course was the point at which access was also gained to the passage through the east range. Inside the archway, the single rib-vaulted bay served as a lobby. The doorway to the passage is to the right.

Directly ahead, the roof is barrel vaulted, and there are two more openings separated by a partition wall. The smaller arch to the left contains a doorway which led out towards a yard at the back of the range. The taller arch to the right accommodated the day stairs to the monks' dormitory. These replaced the earlier stairs, situated next to the parlour, within the east range (p. 52). The ends of some of the steps remain as fragments. Walking through the archway, you will see that the roof was graduated to a higher level to allow for headroom on the stairs. Just outside, high up to the right, a single jamb stone of the doorway into the dormitory still survives.

Warming House

The next doorway in the north range leads into the warming house, a fine vaulted chamber with a great central fireplace. This was the only place in the monastery — apart from the kitchen and infirmary — where a fire was permitted. It was kept burning from 1 November until Good Friday. During these winter months, the monks could restore the circulation to their chilled limbs after hours spent in the cold of the cloister and the church. The Cistercians also used the warming house on occasions for bloodletting (the *seyney*), a highly regarded form of therapy even for healthy monks.

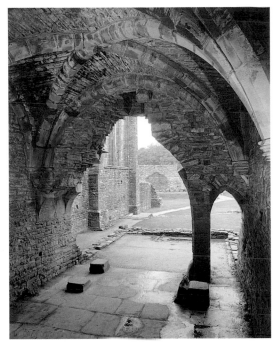

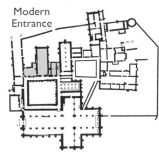

Modern Entrance

Left: The vault survives over the southern half of the warming house.

Below: An impression of the warming house, the room where a fire was kept burning from 1 November to Good Friday (Illustration by Terry Ball, 1995).

In this early thirteenth-century manuscript from Dore Abbey, a monk is shown receiving a tonsure. The tonsure was symbolic of a monk's service of God. The cutting or shaving of hair in this way may have been carried out in the warming house (© The British Library Board, Cotton Cleopatra Ms. C XI, f. 27v).

Beards might be trimmed here, too; hair was periodically clipped for the tonsure (the shaved part of a monk's head); boots were greased; and washed clothes hung up to dry.

The fireplace itself was supported on four square pillars, only one of which survives complete. These supported huge lintels and a tapering hooded cowl. One of the supports for the lintels and some of the edging quoins for the cowl survive on the northern side. Arched passageways to the left and right of the fireplace allowed the monks to huddle around the flames on all sides. North of the fireplace, the room extended beyond the upper floors. This area had a projecting gabled roof whose line can be readily seen as creasing against the face of the building. Fuel for the fire was probably stored in the yard outside. It seems that in later centuries the central fireplace went out of use. The chimney was blocked, and a new smaller fireplace was built at the north end of the room.

The two levels above the warming house are no longer accessible. On the first floor, however, there are two rooms. The larger of these, to the east, has three small windows overlooking the cloister, and two looking north. The smaller, inner room has a stone-vaulted ceiling. Both rooms were probably reached via the day stair and the dormitory. The more secure inner chamber may have served as a muniment room, where the abbey's estate deeds and other important documents could be stored in a safe and dry environment. The larger room may have been an apartment for the prior. Here he could oversee access to the muniment room and ensure that good order was kept in the dormitory.

Late in the abbey's history, a second storey was added above these rooms. The most prominent features at this level are the characteristic Tudor-style square-headed windows. Two three-light examples and one of a single light survive on the north side. There is another single light opening to the south, with the jambs of further windows surviving. As a whole, this well-appointed space must have provided domestic accommodation. If not for one of the senior monks at the time, then it was perhaps intended for a corrodian of the house. It may also have been occupied after the suppression of the abbey.

The Cistercian day was centred around the Rule of St Benedict. *'So intent are they on their Rule' wrote William of Malmesbury, 'they think no jot or tittle of it should be disregarded'. This copy of the* Rule, *from the Cistercian abbey of Zwettl in Austria, dates from about 1173 (Stiftsbibliothek Zwettl, Ms. 84, f. 123v).*

The Monastic Day

It is difficult to provide a precise timetable for a Cistercian monastic day, the daily *horarium*. Custom varied over the centuries, and the arrangements altered with the seasons of summer and winter, and between fasting days and others. Essentially, as a guiding principle, all occupations of the monastic day were to be completed between the rising and the setting of the sun. This table presents no more than an indication of 'typical' days in the earlier medieval centuries.

Summer		Winter	
1.30 a.m.	Rise	2.30 a.m.	Rise
2.00 a.m.	*Nocturns* (later *Matins*)	3.30 a.m.	*Nocturns* (later *Matins*)
3.30 a.m.	*Matins* (*Lauds*)		Reading
	Rest — Reading	6.00 a.m	*Matins* (*Lauds*)
6.00 a.m.	*Prime*		*Prime*
	Chapter Meeting		Reading
	Work	8.00 a.m.	*Terce*
8.00 a.m.	*Terce*		Mass
	Mass		Chapter Meeting
	Reading		Work
11.30 a.m.	*Sext*	12.00 noon	*Sext*
	Dinner		Mass
	Rest	1.30 p.m.	*None*
	Work		Dinner
2.30 p.m.	*None*		Work
	Work	4.15 p.m.	*Vespers*
	Supper		*Collation*
6.00 p.m.	*Vespers*	6.15 p.m.	*Compline*
	Collation	6.30 p.m.	Retire to Bed
8.00 p.m.	*Compline*		
8.15 p.m.	Retire to Bed		

The scale and grandeur of the refectory is captured in this reconstruction of the room in the late thirteenth century. The internal window arcade gave an altogether richer appearance. The form of the roof is conjectural (Illustration by Terry Ball, 1995).

The Monks' Refectory

At the centre of the north cloister alley, a large and once highly decorative doorway opens into the monks' refectory or dining hall. The doorway was the centrepiece of a rather grand facade, all with richly moulded detail, and with clustered arrangements of coursed and detached shafts. Flanking the doorway were the arched recesses of the laver (*lavatorium*). The larger outer arches contained lead- or pewter-lined troughs where the monks washed their hands before going into the refectory for meals. The smaller inner arches probably held towels. The troughs were doubtless supplied with fresh running water from lead pipes fitted with taps.

Every Saturday, and on Maundy Thursday, the laver was used for the *mandatum fratrum*, a ceremonial washing of feet. In this, the monks were emulating the rite instituted by Christ at the Last Supper. It was at the laver, too, that the far more mundane task of laundry washing was undertaken, with the wet clothes probably taken to the warming house to dry.

Inside, the scale of the refectory can be deceptive. At some 84 feet (26m) long and 29 feet (9m) wide, it was a room of quite grand proportions and decorative splendour. It shows an early and dramatic departure from the austerity of initial Cistercian ideals. As much as was possible, the building was flooded with light. On the east side, two pairs of the large four-light windows survive, with much of their heavy external plate tracery. But along the inner edge of the window sills, there was a far more delicate arcade of moulded arches and clustered colonnettes repeating the general pattern of lights. This would have given an altogether more refined appearance to the window openings. Each pair of windows marks a bay division, with a similar arrangement continuing in the more ruinous north end of the refectory. In the southern bay, the inner decorative arcade was carried through as wall panelling. The rhythm of the bay divisions may also have been reflected in the form of the wooden roof.

For much of the year, the monks ate only one main meal a day. They gathered in the refectory about midday, occupying benches set along the

The monks' refectory was a room of considerable architectural grandeur. It provided an appropriate setting for meals which were eaten according to a carefully orchestrated routine.

side walls and facing wooden tables. The prior, who presided over the meal, sat with the senior monks on a dais or high table at the end furthest from the cloister. Until the fourteenth century, meat was officially excluded from the monks' diet, and broadly their meals consisted of bread, two vegetable dishes, with perhaps beans and leeks as a staple. On feast days, fish from the Wye, together with eggs and cheese, made for variety. A generous allowance of

beer was consumed with the meal. Indeed, up to a gallon (4.5 litres) might be drunk daily by each monk, providing an estimated 25 per cent of his average energy requirement.

Meals were taken in silence, broken only by readings from the Bible or other edifying texts. The reader took his place in a projecting pulpit housed in the west wall. Steps led up to the fine little pointed doorway which gave access to the pulpit.

In the south-east corner of the refectory, a door leads to a small vaulted pantry or storeroom. Close by, in the south wall, there are two recesses. That on the left, equipped with a drain and a shelf, was for washing plates and spoons. The second recess has a rebate for a door, and served as a cupboard to store the items.

At the other side of the entrance, in the south end of the west wall, there is a serving hatch from the kitchen, not unlike a modern dining room arrangement. Nearby there is a shallow recess which housed a drop-down table on which dishes coming through from the kitchen could be rested.

Kitchen

To the west of the refectory, the remainder of the north range was occupied by the kitchen. It was positioned so that meals could be served directly to both the choir monks and the lay brothers. Unfortunately, the internal layout was much destroyed by a post-medieval cottage on the site.

However, excavations early in the twentieth century revealed a cross-wall running north to south, dividing the building into two rooms. The smaller eastern room, with a doorway to the cloister, was probably used as the servery. The hatch links through to the refectory. North of this, beyond the modern fence, you will see a chute for carrying out waste into the abbey drain.

The larger room to the west was probably the kitchen proper. It was fitted with three doorways. One of these led to the cloister, another was used to carry food through to the lay brothers in the west range, and the third led out to a kitchen yard to the north. A single cupboard survives in the north-west corner. Wood was probably stored in the kitchen yard and carried through to a large fireplace positioned in the now lost dividing wall. The east wall of the kitchen extends northwards over the drain and may have formed part of a scullery.

The West Range

During the earlier Middle Ages, the west range of cloister buildings in Cistercian monasteries provided segregated accommodation for the *conversi* or lay brethren. Literally converts, coming to the monastic life as adults, these men provided the very backbone of the white monk economy, far outnumbering the choir monks in early centuries.

The Lay Brothers' Refectory and Dormitory

Initially, there was no direct access from the cloister to the lay brothers' accommodation. Later, a skew-passage was formed in the north-west corner of the garth. It leads into a long and relatively narrow range, the northern part of which is now very ruinous. Much of this ground-floor area would have served as the lay brothers' refectory. Meals were brought in from the kitchen via a doorway in the east wall.

At the southern end of the range, where the masonry survives to a greater height, there are two trefoil-headed lancet windows in the west wall, one to each bay. Above these, there is the line of a broad stone vault which covered the refectory space. Overhead, the upper floor was occupied by the lay brothers' dormitory.

The main abbey drain runs below the range, and just to the north of this are the remains of a probable twelfth-century doorway. Its threshold is now barely discernible, but was apparently lower than the floor levels in the thirteenth-century refectory hall; it doubtless belongs to an earlier phase in the layout of the stone monastery. Alongside this doorway, the east wall of the range shows signs of poor construction, with a distinct change in alignment.

North of these features, the low wall which spans the width of the range does not mark the original end of the building; it clearly extended further. To the west, there is a well-defined change in the character of the external masonry at the point where the wall level drops. This indicates more than one phase in construction, and it would seem that

in the thirteenth century the west range was a good deal larger than it may now appear.

It is possible that the range continued beyond the current boundary wall. In such a long building, part of the ground-floor space may have provided a day room for the lay brethren. The northern extension could even have housed the lay brothers' infirmary. If not, then their infirmary presumably lies buried to the west. The lay brothers' latrine must also have stood to the west of the range.

In the second half of the fourteenth century, the demise of the lay brethren meant the original functions of the west range were to become redundant. The northern part may even have been demolished. Alternate uses would have been found for the sections which continued to be maintained. We can only guess at these, though examples of private apartments, storage and even agricultural uses are all known from other Cistercian houses.

To the south of the lay brothers' accommodation there is a square chamber, which was vaulted, and had no direct opening to the cloister. There is a doorway in the north wall, with a doorway and a small window on the west side. The chamber appears to have been used as cellarage.

Porch and Outer Parlour

At the southern end of the west range there is a mid- to late thirteenth-century porch. This was the point at which medieval visitors approached the inner parts of the monastery. Inside, the porch has a stone bench on its south side and a large arched recess to the north. In the fifteenth century, the inner

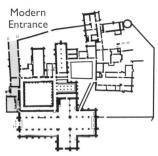

A view looking south along the surviving remains of the west range. Initially, the lay brothers' refectory was on the ground floor with their dormitory above.

A Cistercian lay brother, depicted in a manuscript of about 1269–70, from the abbey of Beaulieu in Hampshire. Over his shoulder, the brother carries a sack, or perhaps a roll of cloth, suggesting he may represent the keeper of the abbey's wool store (© The British Library Board, Additional Ms. 48978, f. 41v).

doorway was rebuilt and a stone vault was added, leading to a greater show of wealth.

Once through the porch, visitors might have been admitted to the outer parlour. Here they were met by members of the community to converse about estate, trade, or other matters. The outer parlour was a vaulted room, with a wide doorway through to the cloister. In the north-west corner, a small doorway gave access to a stair leading to the two rooms above the porch and outer parlour. These formed the cellarer's office and lodging. From here, this senior monastic official could ensure good order among the lay brothers. He would also be on hand to represent the house on business and estate concerns when visitors arrived below.

In the south wall of the outer parlour, a large door opened on to a covered walk by which the lay brothers reached the abbey church. On the east side of the walk are the remains of the stairway which led down from their dormitory to the entrance in the north-west corner of the church. From this point, looking north towards the southern wall of the cellarer's lodging, you will see the remains of a thirteenth-century window, partially blocked, with a smaller fourteenth-century window inserted. The small court in this area probably served as the lay brothers' cloister. In the north-east corner, there are the remains of a stone tank for water storage.

Above: The abbey cellarer's duties included the provision of food and drink to the refectory table. At Tintern his office was in the west range. This humorous manuscript illustration shows a cellarer sampling a brew (© The British Library Board, Sloane Ms. 2435, f. 44v).

Right: The porch and outer parlour at the southern end of the west range.

The Infirmary

The infirmary was essentially reserved for both the sick and aged monks, and for good practical, spiritual and medical reasons it tended to lie in the most secluded part of a medieval monastery. The regimes adopted for sick monks is an area full of potential interest, though rarely does any precise detail survive. At Tintern, we know that general sick care was early regarded as important, both to the community, and in the minds of patrons. About 1240, Gilbert Marshal (d. 1241) granted the abbey 'both shoulders from all deer taken in the park of Trelleck for the use of sick brethren dwelling in that house'.

At the time, the Tintern infirmary may still have been a timber structure. But in the mid- to late thirteenth century, the early medieval buildings were replaced in stone. At the centre of the new complex was a highly impressive aisled hall.

Infirmary Hall

Unfortunately, the hall does not survive to any great height, and it is perhaps difficult to appreciate from the ruins that in origin it was probably one of the most attractive buildings in the abbey complex. Certainly when first built, it would have appeared very much like a church. There was a great central nave, with an aisle to either side, the whole measuring some 107 feet (33m) long and 54 feet (16m) wide. The lavish scale of the construction says much about the importance of spaciousness and generous lighting in medieval medicinal theory, in which corrupted air was seen as a major contributing factor to illness.

The doorway into the hall from the cloister was refashioned in the fourteenth century, in a scheme creating a grander approach by way of a covered passage to the rebuilt abbey church. Inside, the aisles were at first divided from the central nave by arcades supported on clustered piers. Each pier had a central column with detached shafts at the cardinal points. In the first bay at either end of the hall, however, the aisles were cut off by solid walls as part of the original plan.

The bays within these aisles were lit by pairs of lancet windows. We know from early excavations

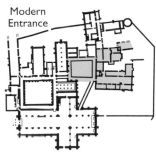

The buildings on the north-east side of the abbey site form two principal groups: the infirmary complex and the abbot's accommodation. The very large infirmary hall stands out as the major feature in the foreground of this view.

that the great east wall was pierced by a much larger window filled with a tracery pattern.

The room extending off the north-west corner has a drain at its northern end. This seems to have been the infirmary latrine. The large chamber at the north-east corner could have served as the infirmarer's lodging. In the late Middle Ages it was equipped with a fireplace. The infirmarer himself was a monk, and in a very general sense a medical practitioner.

The beds were arranged in the aisles. Here, some of the monks cared for may have had acute or chronic illness, others may have become too old to endure the rigours of daily life in the cloister, and some were allowed time here to convalesce. The hall was probably kept warm in winter with portable braziers, and the inmates were given more delicate and nourishing food than the normal monastic diet. Gilbert Marshal's grant of 1240 shows that flesh-meat might have been served quite regularly.

The need for privacy doubtless led to early divisions in the aisle wards. If not wooden partitions, then hangings would have been introduced. In the fifteenth century, screen walls were built to separate the aisles from the central nave. Private cells were created in the walled-off bays, and these were fitted with a fireplace and a small bedside cupboard or locker.

By this time, the sick were probably struggling to maintain a foothold in the infirmary hall. Senior monks probably found the conditions here more desirable than in the draughty communal cloister buildings. Corrodians, too, were perhaps occasionally housed in the infirmary.

Infirmaries were generally provided with their own chapel, and William Worcestre mentioned the existence of one at Tintern in the fifteenth century, though no trace survives today. We cannot be sure, for example, that the chapel was not contained within the infirmary hall itself.

Fireplaces and adjacent cupboards were inserted into the aisles in fifteenth-century modifications to the infirmary. Private cells were created for the comfort of inmates.

A cutaway reconstruction of the infirmary hall as it may have appeared in the late thirteenth century. The placement of a chapel at the east end is conjectural (Illustration by Terry Ball, 1995).

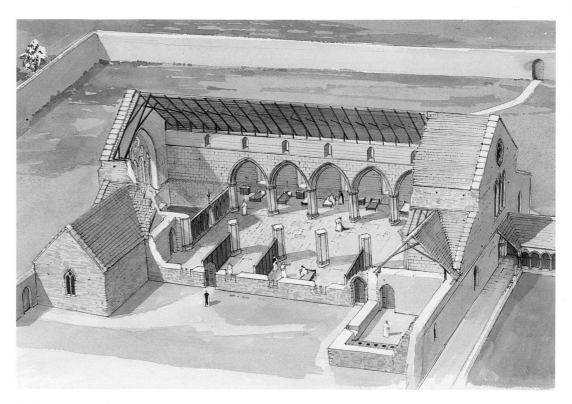

The massive lintel for one of the infirmary kitchen fireplaces lies broken in two in front of the hearth. In the later Middle Ages, the kitchens in this area were probably serving the abbot's hall, as well as senior monks and corrodians who had taken up residence in the infirmary.

Infirmary Cloister and Garden

The gradual development of the infirmary buildings gave rise to a second cloister court, measuring some 84 by 71 feet (26 by 22m). The columns supporting the surrounding arcade were possibly solid paired shafts of a 'dumb-bell' design. The cloister would have provided a space for the convalescents to take the air, and admire the central garden.

Somewhere in the vicinity of the infirmary, perhaps to the north and east, there would have been a well-stocked garden. A wide range of plants for the infirmarer's medicines and cordials would have been grown at the abbey.

Infirmary Kitchen

In the north-east corner of the infirmary cloister, a few steps lead down to a very extensive kitchen complex. This was apparently begun in its present form in the earlier fifteenth century, though may have replaced an earlier structure. In the initial block, you will see the position of the fireplace alongside the northern slabbed floor. The massive lintel rests broken in two in front of the hearth.

Later in the century, another kitchen was added to the east side. The two chambers were connected by a passage to the south. The new wing had two more great fireplaces, one in its east wall and one in its west. The door to the south opened towards the infirmary hall. The northern room, with its slabbed floor intact, was a scullery. To the north-east are the foundations of a probable fourteenth-century building which must have been destroyed or adapted when the later kitchen was built.

These new kitchens were probably built not only in response to demands for higher standards in the infirmary, but also to serve the corrodians and senior monks who had taken up residence in various rooms in this part of the monastery. Not least, the kitchens would also have been designed to provide meals for the abbot's hall and private chamber. Dishes could also have been prepared for the misericord. This was the separate refectory or dining room where the monks were allowed to eat meat (p. 36), which may have existed in this area.

The Abbot's Residence

The remaining buildings to the north-east of the infirmary cloister are best considered as various elements of the abbot's residence. In the twelfth century, in accordance with the *Rule of St Benedict*, the abbot may have slept with his brothers in the common dormitory. But from the first half of the thirteenth century he appears to have acquired separate accommodation (p. 31).

Early Buildings

The earliest discrete apartment for the abbot was probably housed in the L-shaped block situated to the east of the monks' latrine, on the north side of the later infirmary cloister. At first-floor level, this would have linked, via the latrine, to the monks' dormitory. In the fourteenth century, a passage was cut through, separating the block from the latrine. The ground floor then comprised two chambers. The smaller of

the two had a fireplace and an apparently raised doorway out to the infirmary cloister. The larger room also had a doorway to the south and there are traces of a window in the north end of its east wall.

By the time the rooms were modified in the fourteenth century, the block was serving as a private apartment for a senior monk or one of the abbey's corrodians.

The other well-preserved two-storey block to the north-east was also constructed in the early thirteenth century. Though we cannot be certain of its initial purpose (p. 31), it was gradually taken over by the abbot. The upper floor provided a private *camera* or living room, set over a sub-vault.

The Later Hall

The growing status and importance of the abbot are reflected in an extensive rebuilding of his quarters during the fourteenth century. By this time his role had come to appear little different from that of any secular landed magnate. Consequently, not only did he feel justified in accepting a certain degree of style and comfort, it was also a matter of pure necessity in order to entertain and accommodate illustrious

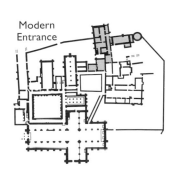

Modern Entrance

The abbot's accommodation was greatly enlarged and extended in the fourteenth century, about 1330–45. This once handsome doorway led on towards a grand upper hall where important guests and visitors were entertained.

A seal of the abbot of Tintern, dating to 1256. Even by this time, the growing status of his office had led to the provision of separate quarters. It was a common pattern throughout the order (© The British Library Board, Harley Charter 75 A. 37, seal 2).

guests and benefactors. In the early decades of the sixteenth century, the complex of buildings at Tintern housed 'the abbot's table', where sat the 'members and gentlemen' of his household. They were attended by six servants in 1535.

The most prominent fourteenth-century addition (perhaps in the 1330s or early 1340s) was a new hall, built on a grand scale, though only the storerooms or cellars of the lower floor can be identified. But even so, these lower levels, with their high-quality mouldings to the numerous doors, and fine corner buttresses, all display confidence with little consideration for cost. The great hall, no doubt with an elaborate timber roof, stood on the upper floor.

On the eastern side of the hall block, there was a lobby with a very fine external door. This may have been approached from a private landing stage on the river. From the lobby, a passage ran down towards a double door at the south-east corner of the building. Meals were probably brought into the hall from the adjacent kitchens via this passage.

Other additions at the time included a chapel block to the south of the abbot's house. The chapel had a two-light east window, and the remains of a piscina survive in the south wall. A latrine was built to communicate with the east side of the upper-floor living chamber. Next to this, the foundations of a circular dovecote were found in excavation. Such buildings were common on later medieval manorial sites, and they are also known from Cistercian abbeys both in Britain and in France.

Further Reading

Acknowledgements

The author is grateful to Dr N. Coldstream, Dr F. G. Cowley, the late Professor R. R. Davies, Mr J. M. Lewis, Mr S. Priestley, Mr R. Turner, Dr D. H. Williams, Professor C. Wilson, and especially Mr W. T. Ball, Mr S. Harrison, Mr C. Jones-Jenkins and Dr R. K. Morris for their kind assistance in the compilation of this guide.

Tintern Abbey

Thomas Blashill, 'The Architectural History of Tintern Abbey', *Transactions of the Bristol and Gloucestershire Archaeological Society*, **6** (1881–82), 88–106.

Harold Brakspear, *Tintern Abbey, Monmouthshire* (HMSO, London 1919; and revised editions 1929, 1934).

Paul Courtney and Madeleine Gray, 'Tintern Abbey after the Dissolution', *Bulletin of the Board of Celtic Studies*, **38** (1991), 145–58.

Paul Courtney, 'Excavations in the Outer Precinct of Tintern Abbey', *Medieval Archaeology*, **33** (1989), 99–143.

O. E. Craster, *Tintern Abbey, Monmouthshire* (HMSO, London 1956).

Julian Harrison, 'The Tintern Abbey Chronicles', *Monmouthshire Antiquary*, **16** (2000), 84–98.

Stuart Harrison, 'The Thirteenth-Century Cloister Arcade at Tintern Abbey', in John R. Kenyon and Diane M. Williams (editors), *Cardiff: Architecture and Archaeology in the Medieval Diocese of Llandaff* (BAA Conference Transaction, **29**, Leeds 2006), 86–101.

Stuart A. Harrison, Richard K. Morris and David M. Robinson, 'A Fourteenth-Century Pulpitum Screen at Tintern Abbey, Monmouthshire', *Antiquaries Journal*, **78** (1998), 177–268.

David M. Robinson, 'The Twelfth-Century Church at Tintern Abbey', *Monmouthshire Antiquary*, **12** (1996), 35–39.

David M. Robinson, 'The Making of a Monument: The Office of Woods and its Successors at Tintern Abbey', *Monmouthshire Antiquary*, **13** (1997), 43–56.

David M. Robinson, 'The Chapter House at Tintern Abbey', *Monmouthshire Antiquary*, **20** (2004), 95–130.

David M. Robinson, *William Wordsworth's Tintern*, sixth edition (Cardiff 2007).

David H. Williams, *White Monks in Gwent and the Border* (Pontypool 1976), 94–146.

The Cistercians

R. A. Donkin, *The Cistercians: Studies in the Geography of Medieval England and Wales* (Toronto 1978).

Peter Fergusson, *Architecture of Solitude: Cistercian Abbeys in Twelfth-Century England* (Princeton 1984).

Peter Fergusson and Stuart Harrison, *Rievaulx Abbey: Community, Architecture, Memory* (New Haven and London 1999)

Christopher Norton and David Park (editors), *Cistercian Art and Architecture in the British Isles* (Cambridge 1986).

David Robinson (editor), *The Cistercian Abbeys of Britain: Far from the Concourse of Men* (London 1998).

David M. Robinson, *The Cistercians in Wales: Architecture and Archaeology 1130–1540* (London 2006).

David H. Williams, *The Welsh Cistercians* (Leominster 2001).

Monastic History and Buildings

Mick Aston, *Monasteries in the Landscape* (Stroud 2000).

Janet Burton, *Monastic and Religious Orders in Britain 1000–1300* (Cambridge 1994).

Glyn Coppack, *Abbeys and Priories* (London 1990).

F. G. Cowley, *The Monastic Order in South Wales 1066–1349* (Cardiff 1977).

J. Patrick Greene, *Medieval Monasteries* (Leicester 1992).

David Knowles, *The Monastic Order in England*, second edition (Cambridge 1963).

C. H. Lawrence, *Medieval Monasticism: Forms of Religious Life in Western Europe in the Middle Ages*, third edition (Harlow 2001).